Marketing
to the Public Sector
and Industry

D1187152

Mergers, Acquisitions and Alternative Corporate Strategies
Hill Samuel Bank Limited

Tax: Strategic Corporate Tax Planning
Price Waterhouse

Finance for Growth
National Westminster Bank PLC

Company Law and Competition
S J Berwin & Co

Marketing: Communicating with the Consumer
D'Arcy Masius Benton & Bowles

Information Technology: The Catalyst for Change
PA Consulting Group

Marketing to the Public Sector and Industry
Rank Xerox Limited

Transport and Distribution
TNT Express

Property
Edward Erdman

Employment and Training
Manpower plc

Marketing
to the Public Sector
and Industry
Rank Xerox Limited

With a Foreword by Richard Ryder, OBE, MP
Paymaster General

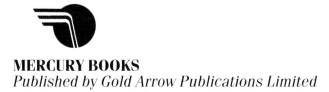

Published in association with
CBI Initiative 1992

MERCURY BOOKS
Published by Gold Arrow Publications Limited

Copyright © Confederation of British Industry 1990

All rights reserved. No part of this publication may be reproduced,
stored in a retrieval system, or transmitted in any form or by any
means, electronic, mechanical, photocopying, recording, or otherwise,
without the prior permission of the publishers.

First published in 1990
by Mercury Books
Gold Arrow Publications Limited
862 Garratt Lane, London SW17 0NB

Set in Plantin by Phoenix Photosetting, Chatham
Printed and bound in Great Britain by
Butler & Tanner Ltd, Frome, Somerset

This book is sold subject to the condition that it shall not,
by way of trade or otherwise, be lent, re-sold, hired out or
otherwise circulated without the publisher's prior consent
in any form of binding or cover other than that in which it
is published and without a similar condition including this
condition being imposed on the subsequent purchaser.

British Library Cataloguing in Publication Data

Marketing to the public sector and industry.
1. Marketing European Economic Countries
I. Rank Xerox   II. CBI Initiative 1992
658.80094

ISBN 1-85251-037-4

Contents

Foreword   vii
Preface   ix

I   Public procurement

1. Liberalising the public sector   3
2. The potential of the public sector   10
3. How the system works – public supplies procedures   21
4. How the system works – public works procedures   28
5. Enforcing the rules   36
6. Broadening the scope   40
7. Sources of information   46

II   Technical barriers to trade

8. Technical barriers and their effect   51
9. The differential impact   55
10. Harmonisation of standards   62

III   Marketing to Europe

11. Achieving the benefits – the reality   77
12. Strategic marketing and the philosophy of change   87
13. Creating a market-led organisation   97
14. Getting the information right   105
15. Market entry – gaining access   116
16. Maintaining competitive advantage   127
17. Product strategy   139
18. Sales strategies and practices   149

Appendices

1. Enforcement – legal cases   163
2. Viewpoints   167
3. Model tender notices   170
4. New approach directives – Toy safety: A case study   176
5. PowerGen: A case study   180
6. Kilco Chemicals: A case study   184

7. BSI standards policy committee groups   187
8. Bibliography   189
9. Contact points   191

Index   195

Foreword

The completion of the single market in public procurement has long been a priority for the United Kingdom. New and improved directives will lead to new challenges and opportunities for purchasers and suppliers alike. The CBI's Initiative 1992 and the series of conferences held in 1989 helped to alert suppliers to the need to be competitive both at home and in seeking out opportunities in other member states. I hope that this book and the associated audio programme will further this important process.

Purchasers affected by the existing or proposed directives also need to keep themselves up to date with developments to ensure that they make arrangements for complying with their obligations. In due course they will need to be aware of the statutory instruments which will be introduced to implement the Compliance Directive and transpose the Works and Supplies Directives into our national law. At a later date we will need to legislate for the utilities sector and for the forthcoming directives on services.

I would like to underline my gratitude to the CBI and its Public Procurement Contact Group for their help in obtaining views on the developing proposals from both sides of industry.

Richard Ryder, OBE, MP
Paymaster General
HM Treasury

Preface

There are radical changes happening now in the areas of public procurement and marketing to industry in Europe, and this book seeks to cover the most important developments which your company will need to address when developing a European marketing strategy.

There are many reasons, both commercial and social, why national preferences have, in the past, taken precedence over economic logic or cost effectiveness in the public procurement market place. The current liberalisation of this market place will have significant potential benefits for the Community as a whole and for any company which is familiar with and prepared for the new regime.

Additionally, companies will find that their strategy for the single market must include a willingness and a capacity to embrace the new standards, regulations testing and certification requirements as they are put in place.

As well as covering the actual changes in some detail, we have aimed to present the essentials of a pragmatic approach to the single market environment. We have emphasised the philosophy behind changing and refocusing organisations so that they become market-led in the wider and more competitive market place. We have aimed to maintain a clear perception of the daily realities while providing a practical reference guide to ideas about, approaches to and the implementation of the relevant strategies. (Readers should note that Chapers 3 and 4 on public supplies and public works should be read in parallel. The information contained in these chapters is similar at first sight but essential differences do exist.)

Rank Xerox Limited has been essentially European since 1956, and our experience of Europe is our first credential for offering this book to British companies. We are delighted to be associated with CBI Initiative 1992.

David Thompson
Chairman
Rank Xerox (UK) Limited

★ This book was completed with information current at 30 September 1990.

I
Public procurement

1. Liberalising the public sector

The rationale for change

Preferential treatment

Public procurement has always been influenced by local or national preferment in the awarding of contracts for the supply of goods or the undertaking of public works and services. The reasons for this preferential treatment of some suppliers in relation to others are not difficult to identify. Often justification exists in their national context, in spite of existing legislation. The objective of the single market programme is to implement policies which reduce or eliminate those preferences which operate on unacceptable criteria or depart from commercial logic, when viewed from the perspective of the Community as a whole.

The case for further EC legislation and for the reinforcement of the current intervention measures is that not only will local and national preferences continue to affect public sector decisions if nothing is done, but also that the effect of such preferences will be to the collective disadvantage of the people who live in the Community.

Where preference is justified

In individual member states, public sector purchasing decisions are not always made simply on the basis of the cheapest option. Decisions are likely to include reference to 'value for money' or some equivalent sentiment which indicates that 'price' often has to be evaluated in terms of quality, product specification and technical standards. In the terminology which has emerged in the Commission directives, contracts are often decided on an evaluation of the 'economically most advantageous' proposition. There are two reasons which might justify preference of particular suppliers to the public sector:

1. Commercial For some public sector purchases, local suppliers have a natural competitive advantage which attracts no criticism or comment. These would include numerous relatively small purchases where the advantage of proximity of location is influential. Such factors could be important where local and frequent deliveries are needed, transport costs are likely to be large, or an after-sales service is part of the deal. Similarly there will be contracts where a language requirement is necessary and would narrow down the number of potential suppliers. These factors point to valid commercially related criteria which can influence the award of supply contracts.

2. Social Many decisions have also been influenced by what may be termed indirect, or social, considerations. *The Cost of Non-Europe in Public Sector Procurement*, a study prepared for the Commission by W. S. Atkins Management Consultants identified a number of the considerations which influence public purchasing decisions. These include strategic reasons (e.g. defence, telecommunications, aerospace); support for employment in declining industries; compensation for local communities near environmentally damaging public industries (e.g. coal mining, nuclear fuels); support for emerging high tech industries; and general political reasons. A cynic might suggest that under such a set of considerations almost any industry, or type of employment, could find justification for preferential treatment.

The single market

On its own, without reinforcing measures, the existence of the single market would not necessarily cause major changes to public procurement practices. The codification of standards and specifications will make cross-frontier purchasing possible in some sectors where it has been impossible, and legislation already exists to encourage more competition in public procurement. However, without further legislation, decisions would continue to be made by national, local or other public agencies without adequate regard to the Community dimension, and a mutually self-defeating 'beggar-my-neighbour' outcome would be the result. Not only might protectionist policies continue to be in evidence, but over time the gulf between the public and private sectors would increase as the private sector enjoys an increasing volume of cross-border trade within the Community as a result of EC competition policy.

Encouraging competition

Public procurement policy has therefore been developed through the acceptance of generally agreed principles and the application of common procedures to ensure a uniform effect between the member states. A regulated framework is needed to ensure that competitive processes will function on agreed principles, using set procedures, to achieve defensible decisions, to the ultimate benefit of the consumer.

Public understanding

Some businesses may feel that such rules, proposed by the Commission and adopted by the Council, are an unwelcome and unnecessary threat to their activities. Businesses and the general public may require some persuasion that the discretionary decision making of local and national public sector agencies should be constrained. A number of arguments is involved:

- A system that does not have an EC-wide set of common rules is unnecessarily expensive

- Such a system is unfair to companies trading across member states

- An equitable, open and competitive market for the public sector requires an EC-wide set of common rules

- An EC-wide approach is needed to achieve the full potential development of the sector across all member states

- The improved system must be reinforced by adequate monitoring of the procedures and a workable system of enforcement, accompanied by appropriate remedies when there is a breach of the rules

Need for regulation

In short, public sector procurement policies in some member states tend currently to be protective of local or national interests. The reasons for this are understandable although they are often based on unsustainable, or short-term, objectives. The completion of the single market, simply as a removal of border obstacles to trade, would be inadequate to widen the source of suppliers for public sector contracts. A regulatory framework is needed to allow equitable conditions to apply to all potential suppliers. This EC-wide system will only be effective if it is accompanied by adequate powers of enforcement including the possibility of remedial action. This is the thrust of the Commission policies, the evolution of which is summarised in the following pages.

Defining the public sector – the problem of ownership

The public sector is very large, and far from homogeneous. Twelve member states using up to ten working languages and with many differing national standards, regulations and specification details, is a long way from the convenience of currency, legal system, language and standards to be found, for example, in the 'single market' of the USA or Japan.

Defining what is in the public sector is very difficult. Obviously central and local government and their agencies – but what about Sealink? The water authorities? British Gas?

In an attempt to codify what is included in the 'public sector' for the purposes of applying procurement rules to the previously excluded sectors of water, energy, transport and telecommunications, the EC has had to find a working definition which is not dependent on the concept of ownership. If the definition were based solely on government ownership, then the privatisation process would have taken (for example) British Telecom and British Gas out of the public sector. These industries are still closely supervised by government-created agencies and have near monopoly powers for their main products.

The Commission has therefore adopted a definition which includes enterprises, whether privately or publicly owned, which, by *monopoly*, *concession* or *licence*, provide a public service. Using this approach, public procurement procedures will be introduced to apply to the gas, electricity, railway and airport companies (even after privatisation). Outside the scope of this definition will be British Airways, British Shipbuilders, British Aerospace and Sealink, all of which are, or were, government-owned but are in competition with other firms over the full range of their output.

The value of the public sector

Market size

The EC estimates that in 1986 the value of purchases and contracts controlled by the public sector was over £350 billion (530 billion ecu). Total sector spending on goods and services, excluding wages and salaries, is 15 per cent of gross domestic product on a Community-wide basis. (In the UK this figure is over 21 per cent of GDP.)

Not all these public sector purchases fall within public procurement procedures. Many transactions (5–8 per cent) are too small to come within contractual procedures. However the remainder of public sector purchases (7–10 per cent of GDP) still represents a considerable number of market opportunities which may be available for more competitive determination on an intra-Community basis.

In 1986 the size of this 'available' market as defined above would have been between £160 and £225 billion (240–340 billion ecu,

Cecchini, 1988). At present, less than 2 per cent of this total goes directly to companies in other member states. Even if imported goods used by local firms are included in this total, it would still amount to less than 10 per cent of the market.

The Atkins Study

The only readily available source of information on the value of public sector purchases subject to contract procurement procedures is the Atkins study (Atkins, 1988). It tried to assemble the available information for five of the EC member states: Belgium, West Germany, Italy, France and the UK.

Variations in purchasing

Using national accounts and technical input–output studies, Atkins compiled estimates for 1984 of the value of public sector purchases in the five selected member states. Out of an EC total which was estimated as about 500 billion ecu, the analysis covers sectors supplying some 384 billion ecu. Because of differences in institutional and structural arrangements, an analysis of where the purchases originated shows different patterns from member state to member state. In France, for example, the decisions on purchasing are very dispersed but with some large and powerful purchasing agencies at the centre. West Germany and Italy operate a highly decentralised system: more so than Belgium which is only moderately decentralised. Interestingly, the UK is the most centralised of this group of five countries.

Public sector purchases in Atkins's study were shown to originate from a variety of sources:

Source	Value (billion ecu)	
Central government	124	Total public administration 227 billion ecu
Local government	96	
Social security administration	7	
Public enterprises	157	
Total	**384**	

Suppliers to the public sector

As was stated earlier, not all supplies to the public sector can be based on contract procedures. Many payments are for routine purchases which are based on individual needs for the supply of goods or services. In addition, many purchases are for non-competitive services such as rents, electricity and travel. Contract procedures are, however, the usual method of reassuring potential suppliers that opportunities are being made available to bid for business. These procedures are also designed to maintain objective standards in the use of public sector finance.

Sectoral breakdown

In the absence of adequate information on the different types of purchasing procedures in operation, Atkins produced estimates of the total value of supplies to the public sector. The largest supplying sector, using this categorisation, is the building and civil engineering industry. At 102 billion ecu, the value of work given to this sector represented 26 per cent of the total. The next largest (9 per cent) was transport equipment (excluding motor vehicles), which is probably dominated by defence-related aerospace spending. Third largest was the purchase of refined petroleum products (8 per cent) and related mainly to the operation of electricity generation. The largest supplying sectors are listed below.

Public sector purchases: supplying sectors (1984)	
Sector	(billion ecu)
Building and civil engineering work	102
Transport equipment (excluding vehicles)	35
Refined petroleum products	31
Electrical goods	18
Business services	18
Coal	14
Chemical products	12
Market services (excluding health and education)	11
Agricultural and industrial machinery	10
Distribution	10
Paper goods and printing	9
Electric power	9
Metal products	9
Credit and insurance	8
Communications	7
Office machines	7
Motor vehicles	7
Property rentals	6
Railway transport	5

[Source: Atkins, Part A, p. 317]

Dependence on the public sector

Many quite small industrial and commercial sectors are heavily dependent upon the public sector to take their output (e.g. coal and lignite). Other sectors may make high value sales to the public sector but, because of the sheer size of the sector, this might be a relatively small percentage of the sector's total output (e.g. business services). The table below lists a range of industrial and commercial sectors in decreasing order of reliance on the public sector.

Public sector purchases as a percentage of gross output of supplying sector (1984) where purchases exceeded 250 million ecu	
Lignite	96
Transport equipment (excluding vehicles)	62
Coal	58
Building and civil engineering	31
Market services of education and research	30
Nuclear fuels	20
Refined petroleum products	16
Railway transport services	16
Water	14
Communications	13
Office machines	13
Electric power	12
Manufactured gases	12
Paper goods and printing	12
Market services	11
Electrical goods	11
Natural gas	11
Business services	10
Air transport services	9
Average (all covered sectors)	8

[Source: Atkins, Part A, p. 319]

Hardly surprisingly, the coal and lignite suppliers come to the top of the list. Of the sales of lignite, 96 per cent went to the public sector as did 58 per cent of the sales of coal. Almost two-thirds (62 per cent) of transport equipment (excluding motor vehicles) was supplied to the public sector, which reflects the links between aerospace and defence supplies. Nearly a third (31 per cent) of the building and civil engineering turnover was for the public sector.

2. The potential of the public sector

Measuring the benefits – the problems

We have established in Chapter 1 that public purchasing is large in each member state of the EC and that it has in the past, to a major degree, been directed to home country sources. The involvement of the Community might therefore be justified simply on the principle of providing equality of opportunity to suppliers and contractors to operate on normal commercial criteria across national boundaries. Providing equality of opportunity, however, will not in itself create major changes in the pattern of public sector spending. Research undertaken by the Commission shows that there are significant **Market distortions** market distortions in the present arrangements which must be removed to produce changes both in the submission of bids by potential suppliers from one member state to another and in the allocation of contracts. Changes are therefore expected as a result of EC legislation, although their impact may be distributed unevenly from sector to sector.

As in all cases where market forces lead to changes, the incidence of the changes cannot be predicted with precision. The response of supplying firms will vary and competitive adjustments will be uneven between firms and sectors. At a macro-economic level, assessments can be made of the areas which are likely to experience pressure for change. The Atkins study attempts to anticipate where these changes may occur. It examines the whole range of public sector purchases to answer the question, 'How would the opening up of the internal Community market affect public sector purchasing decisions and how would it affect the suppliers?' (As a supplementary and more technical issue, the study postulates that public sector imports in an open market might rise significantly higher and asks whether competitive forces might not raise this ratio nearer to the level which has emerged in the private sector.)

Savings

The Atkins study suggests that as a result of single market legislation the goods and services bought by the public sector might:

- Be cheaper, by costing 17.5 billion ecu less (at 1986 prices)

- Be the equivalent of a price reduction of about 3 per cent in the total costs to the public sector of its supplies

- Represent a gain of about 0.5 per cent of EC GDP.

These figures are obviously general estimates. In the full report they are quoted within ranges of possibilities which emerge from sensitivity analyses, allowing for variations in the underlying assumptions.

Where do the savings come from?

The differing effects of the opening up of the internal market have been identified as arising in three ways:

1. Price effect First, there is the consequence for the public sector of having a greater choice of supply sources. For some purchases there will be alternative sources which are cheaper. These commodities have enough of a price difference to merit cross-border purchasing. The study refers to this as the price effect. Clearly those sectors and products which will benefit under this criterion are those which have a large share in public purchasing and might potentially lead to significant savings; are tradeable; are not currently freely traded; and benefit at present from differing degrees of domestic market protection, for whatever reason. However, even if your product or service fits this refined list, price comparisons are sometimes difficult to make. This is because prices often vary within a country as well as between countries; there continue to be differences in standards, quality and specifications which can be an indirect or concealed factor in price differences; at any given date, comparisons need to use an appropriate exchange rate, but these are subject to variations which would affect price comparisons; and because even when comparable prices can be estimated, allowance for transport cost (and other costs of trade affecting value for money) must be made and assessed in estimating possible savings.

2. Competition effect The second set of consequences of the opening up of the market arises as a result of the competitive process. If a supplier thinks a contract may be lost because of the appearance of other possible suppliers, the supplier may offer to supply at a lower price and operate on a lower profit margin. The study refers to this as the competition effect.

3. Restructuring effect The new market opportunities will bring long-term structural changes as different sectors rationalise capacity to exploit the economies of scale of the larger market. The greatest potential for such change lies with firms who cannot at present exploit economies of scale because the nature of the fragmented market means that production units are smaller than the optimum. This is more likely where a large part of the output from the industry is already sold to the public sector. This third type of change is more difficult to quantify than it is to specify. In the study this is called the restructuring effect.

Win or lose – which sectors?

Price and competition effects The following sectors were identified by Atkins as worthy of further consideration of the price and competition effects because they matched the profile outlined above.

Sector	Share in public purchasing (%)
Aerospace equipment, arms	6.8
Pharmaceuticals	1.6
'Other' mechanical engineering	1.3
Power generating equipment	0.9
Shipbuilding	0.9
Telecom, electro-medical equipment	0.9
Coal for power stations	3.7
Computer equipment	0.9
Motor vehicles	1.7
Power cables	0.5
Office and street lighting	0.5
Railway rolling stock	0.9
Heavy steel fabrications	1.2
Explosives	0.3
School and office desks, furniture	0.7
Uniforms and clothing	0.7
Paper	0.4
Cement	0.05
HVAC equipment	0.1
Nuclear fuels	0.3
Special civil engineering	2.7
Business services	4.6

[Source: Atkins p. 30]

This estimate of the share in public sector spending is reached after adjustment for the proportion of goods or services which enter the new, potentially competitive arena. The full list is estimated to cover about a third of all public procurement. (Not all these sectors will be covered by the EC public procurement legislation: the purchase of fuel by energy producers is, for example, not included at present.) This list of sectors was further refined to include only those where standard products could be used to make price comparisons easier. Further enquiries were made on specific products in the five member **Winners and losers** states in the study. In the resulting table, the two columns to the right show, first, the member state which seemed to be the potential supplier of cheaper products to one or more of the others and, second, which member state, if any, might benefit most from lower prices.

Product	Supplier	Purchaser
Pharmaceuticals	France	W. Germany
Cars and vans	Belgium	France
Electrical office equipment*	Belgium	Italy
Power cables	UK	Belgium
Street lighting	UK	Belgium
Office lighting	France	–
School desks	UK	–
Office desks and furniture	Italy	W. Germany
Filing cabinets and shelves	UK	W. Germany
Uniforms	W. Germany	Belgium
Paper	Italy	W. Germany
Cement	Italy	–
Electro-medical equipment	UK	Italy
Telephones	Italy/UK	France
Railway wagons	France	W. Germany
Electrical transformers	Italy	UK

* The commodity used to assess office equipment was an electric typewriter. The results vary from product to product.

Restructuring effects

The sectors which will be affected by restructuring effects are those which are heavily dependent on the public sector; contain only a small number of big producers; operate in a monopolistic or oligopolistic market, and might be regarded as 'national champions'. The main examples are coal, iron and steel tubes and special steels, heavy steel fabrication, power generation equipment (including electric rail locomotives), shipbuilding and railway rolling stock; and, in what might

13

be termed modern industries, nuclear fuel processing, computers, telecommunications, optoelectronics (specifically lasers), aircraft and avionics.

The following thumbnail analyses indicate some of the issues facing a selection of industries which will feed the 'restructuring effect'.

1. Coal (Current proposals do not include the procurement of coal by energy producers.) This may need to be treated as a special sector because of the obligations under the European Coal and Steel Community (ECSC). Left to market forces, production in West Germany and the UK would be reduced because of the importing of alternative supplies. Big price falls could occur in both countries and accelerate closure of 10 per cent of UK pits and most German pits.

2. Heavy fabrications (boilers and pressure vessels) World over-capacity. Capacity utilisation in EC about 30 per cent which points to the opportunity for short-term economies of scale. A more open market will increase import penetration, encourage mergers and/or closures, lead to price reduction of up to 20 per cent, increased product specialisation and a monopoly for France in PWR technology. These changes may be inevitable and there may be a reduction in employment. Opening the EC market may ease the adaptation process and create a sustainable EC sector.

3. Turbine generators Present capacity is being absorbed by the revival of power station contracts. Possible fall in prices of 10 per cent. An open internal market should encourage improved capacity utilisation between all EC firms. Rationalisation between EC firms and other European firms is expected. French and West German firms may become additional suppliers to the UK and Italy.

4. Electric locomotives Possible increase in imports of diesel locomotives from the USA, Japan and Korea. Price competition may reduce prices in Belgium, West Germany and Italy by 20–30 per cent; not in France and the UK. If the market remained static, then rationalisation would be needed. However, the market may expand. The number of main manufacturers may reduce from sixteen to about three or four. These changes are forecast because of changing technology; they will be facilitated by the opening up of public procurement.

5. Mainframe computers A growing market sector may possibly grow by 10 per cent per annum. EC manufacturers may lose market share to US and Japanese firms. This effect may be more noticeable in France where the market is more protected. EC's four main manufacturers may increase their collaboration. Export performance may improve. A long-term equivalent of a 5 per cent price reduction is suggested.

6. Telecommunications (public exchange switching equipment)   Opening up the EC market is expected to be accompanied by significant price reductions (30–70 per cent). There is expected to be a reduction in the number of EC suppliers and big economies of scale for the remaining factories. Some increase in imports from 8 per cent to about 20 per cent is expected as is an increase in exports.

7. Telephone handsets   Prices are likely to fall in France, West Germany and Belgium by 25–40 per cent. However an increase in imports will create pressure to restructure and the number of manufacturers may fall. Product range may narrow and focus on new technology. Import penetration will rise and the surviving EC firms may gain increased exports in a growing total market.

8. Lasers   A high tech product but one where the market is (with marginal reservations about France) thought to be fairly open already.

Potential savings – how much?

The potential savings are calculated by applying the sectoral assessments to the three categories discussed earlier: price, competition and restructuring effects.

The price effect is prepared by applying the anticipated price changes to the appropriate category. For the group of five member states in the study, covering some 80 per cent of the possible EC total, the total price effect in 1984 was 6.6 billion ecu. It had the following components:

Sector	Five member states (billion ecu)	UK only (billion ecu)
Coal	2.1	0.2
Chemical products	1.0	0.4
Agricultural and industrial machinery	0.1	0.03
Office machines	0.2	0.07
Electrical goods	0.4	0.1
Motor vehicles	0.08	0.04
Other transport equipment	1.2	0.2
Textile and clothing	0.1	neg
Building and civil engineering	1.0	0.2
Business services	0.2	0.05
Total (after rounding)	6.6*	1.4

* Belgium 0.5, France 0.4, West Germany 3.1 (coal = 1.8), Italy 1.2, UK 1.4.

While there may be effects elsewhere, analysis points to the biggest impact of competition and restructuring effects falling in two sectors: electrical goods (which is mainly capital investment) and other transport equipment (which includes aircraft, ships and railway locomotives).

Sector	Competition (billion ecu)	Restructuring (billion ecu)	Total (billion ecu)
Electrical goods	0.9	0.8	1.7
Other transport equipment	1.0	5.2	6.2
Total	1.9	6.0	7.9

Summary of potential savings

For the five member states in the special study, the potential savings were added together, giving the following result:

	(billion ecu)
Price effect	6.6
Competition effect	1.9
Restructuring effect	6.0
Total	14.5

of which the UK's share was 3.8 billion ecu.

The main value of this analysis is to identify sectors and products which may be subject to change as a consequence of opening up the market for public sector procurement. The quantification of the possible scale of the price changes to the public sector customers is of interest but should be treated as estimated. There are however a number of qualitative comments which are appropriate:

The analysis assumes that the internal market is indeed open to suppliers across the Community and from outside, and that no barriers remain (no cartels, no market sharing, no exclusive dealerships, no separate national standards, no trade formalities and no indirect deterrent through product approval procedural requirements). This means that the estimates may be too high – it is unlikely that such an entirely free market will ever exist. A further bias is the inevitable inclusion of some changes that would happen even if the public procurement market were not changed by Community legislation – the growth of natural competition.

Nevertheless, this process should undoubtedly strengthen the position of EC firms in 'third' markets in competition with the USA and Japan. In addition, beneficial dynamic effects of the changes (through more effective research and development spending) will have some knock-on effects for private sector purchasing.

Early decisions

The logic of a more open public procurement policy has been accepted in the EC since its inception. Such a policy is an essential component of a single market and a reciprocal of other policies, such as:

- Encouraging competition

- Controlling the abuse of market position by large organisations

- Avoiding distortion in the market-place by the use of state aids to industry.

The Commission took the first steps to formalise Community policy in the early 1970s. Legislative action developed in the form of directives rather than regulations. Directives are 'binding as to the result to be achieved but shall leave the national authorities choice of form and method', whereas regulations have direct application as law in each member state.

Measures and principles

Specific measures

The Commission has evolved different requirements for the different sorts of purchases made by public authorities. Directives already agreed have set out separate requirements for public works (i.e. construction and civil engineering) and the procurement of supplies (i.e. goods). The earliest directive was published in 1971 and related to public works. This was followed in 1977 by a directive on government procurement of supplies of goods and equipment. Both directives have been amended since then but they outlined the fundamental principles which underpin Commission policy. The most recent changes (to supplies in 1988 and to works in 1989) have strengthened the procedures and clarified the coverage of the directives.

More recent proposals apply similar rules to public enterprises which were excluded from the existing Works Directive and Supplies Directive (i.e. water, energy, transport and telecommunications – the 'excluded sectors') and to services. The proposal on the excluded sectors has recently been agreed by the Council. A proposal on services is still awaited.

Principles

The general principles are that:

- Suppliers from all EC member states should have an equal opportunity to bid for public authority contracts. (This implies that firms in any member state should have the right to set up in business in any other member state, although this is not specified in the directive.)

- Tendering and award-making procedures should be clear and available to all potential suppliers.

- Firms not resident in the EC should not be subject to discrimination, but should have equal opportunities with EC-based firms, although this principle is also not explicit in the directive.

The earlier steps in 1971 and 1977, can, with hindsight, be seen to have been too modest in their content and in the manner of their implementation. The objectives in the earlier directives were that:

- Contracts should be determined by an open competitive tendering procedure. Negotiated or single tenders were to be the exception only in specified circumstances.

- The use of technical specifications as a form of discrimination was to be prohibited.

- Tenders above a minimum price were to be advertised in the *Official Journal of the European Communities*, together with a minimum set of time periods to give adequate opportunity for the submission of a bid.

- Certain types of public enterprise were excluded. As stated earlier these related to public water supplies, energy providers, public transport and some telecom services. (These exceptions will end when the Utilities Directive is brought into force.)

GATT

An added reason for this codification of public purchasing procedures was the acceptance by the EC of an obligation imposed on all member states under the Government Procurement Agreement of the General Agreement on Tariffs and Trade (GATT). This obliged governments not to discriminate against external suppliers when central government or its agencies are purchasing supplies. The 1977 Supplies Directive was amended in 1980 to incorporate the GATT requirements. Further changes to broaden the range of contracts covered and to set lower minimum value thresholds for central government purchases as agreed in GATT were introduced in early 1988.

Successes and failures

The success of the 1971 Works Directive and the 1977 Supplies Directive lay in introducing a Community-wide procedure and gaining acceptance of the need to advertise contract opportunities. However, the opinion of the Commission was that the effects of the legislation were disappointing. A number of possible weaknesses were identified. These include:

- Inadequate efforts to enforce the requirements

- Inadequate remedial mechanisms

- Too many excluded sectors

- Failure by some authorities to advertise for some contracts

- Abuse of the exceptions on single or negotiated tendering

- Various forms of discrimination through administrative, financial, or technical requirements

- Illegal disqualification of bidders (e.g. by the use of discriminatory selection criteria)

The regulative position in mid 1990

The Commission acknowledged the need for new, additional directives to guarantee acceptable public procurement practices, as well as the need to ensure that the rules are observed, and corrective action taken where faults are identified.

- A new directive on the public procurement of supplies and equipment was adopted on 22 March 1988 and came into force in the UK on 1 January 1989.

- A new directive on public works and construction, to parallel that on supplies, was adopted on 18 July 1989 and brought into force in the UK on 18 July 1990.

- A directive to provide remedies to correct, or compensate for, faults in the public procurement systems of public authorities as they affect potential suppliers was adopted on 21 December 1989 and is due to be brought into force in the UK by 1 December 1991.

- A directive on procurement procedures as applied to enterprises providing water, energy and transport services and telecommunications was adopted on 17 September 1990 to be brought into force in the UK by 1 January 1993.

- Discussion papers on a proposal for a directive on the purchase of services by the public sector are being considered.

3. How the system works – public supplies procedures

The public sector supplies procedures in the EC are now governed by two main directives, the scope of which is limited to public authorities. These are 77/62/EEC (adopted in 1977) and 88/295/EEC (adopted in mid 1988). To take advantage of the opening of the market to allow bids to be submitted by suppliers throughout the EC, these documents set out the way in which the system is to work. A consolidated directive to replace the original directives and provide the detail in a single document is expected in due course.

The requirements of Community legislation are a necessary element in the understanding of the mechanisms for the allocation of contracts. However, these are supplementary to, and not a substitute for, knowledge of the national, local or public sector enterprise in the target market and information on the procurement procedures and rules that apply. The importance of such local knowledge is further discussed in the later sections of this book.

Local procedures As you will see, national and local information can be obtained from diverse sources. Specialist suppliers will need to obtain information on the relevant market, the main users and the competitive suppliers who already have the advantage of such local knowledge. Some helpful guidance on the institutional arrangements in each member state is available in the Annexes to the GATT Government Procurement Agreement published by the GATT Secretariat (DG I Directorate A, European Commission, Rue de la Loi 200, 1049 Brussels). There is information on the institutional structure in Belgium, France, West Germany, Italy and the UK in the Atkins study (Part A, pp. 92–177). Further details on the national procedures for these five member states and the value of procurements by the different agencies in 1984 are also provided by Atkins (Part A, pp. 178–309).

Community legislation is designed to help all potential suppliers to have better information and procedural reassurances on fairness. Directive 88/295/EEC is now in force for nine of the member states. In Greece, Spain and Portugal, the directive will become effective in 1992. It covers all supplies to public authorities, but does not include public enterprises (the excluded sectors).

The rules

The following paragraphs give a broad summary of the EC rules which apply to public supply tenders. A list of information sources for more details is to be found in Appendix 9. It is essential that tenders are correct and complete down to the smallest details and if in doubt appropriate professional advice should always be sought.

Advertising

Public supplies contracts above a certain threshold must be advertised in the *Official Journal of the European Communities* (the OJ). The information in the OJ is also made available through the Tenders Electronic Daily (TED) database. Further information on this database is given in Chapter 7.

Contract authorities

A public supply contract may be defined as 'a contract for pecuniary consideration concluded in writing between a supplier and a contracting authority (purchasing or procurement agency) for the supply of products'. The contract may also include siting and installation work. Procurement is defined now to include either outright purchase or leasing, rental or hire purchase. Lists of 'contracting authorities' are published for each country. Broadly, the authorities include all government departments, local government, and publicly controlled education, health, police and housing bodies.

Exclusions

There are five general categories of excluded contracts:

1. Most *public sector trading utilities* are still outside the scope of the directives.

2. *Small contracts* are excluded. These are less likely to be of interest on a cross-border basis and their exclusion removes a large amount of information from the system which would only infrequently be of value to external suppliers. The limit set for small contracts in 1988 was 200,000 ecu (about £141,000).

    The small contracts limit for central government supplies where the GATT code applies was 134,000 ecu (or £94,000) in January 1990. (These rates are set using the average exchange rates in the two years up to the previous November and are published in the OJ.)

3. Procurement linked to *awards made under international agreements* between an EC member state and a non-EC country where there is a joint project, possibly related to development aid, is excluded, as are contracts to supply international agencies.

4. Products for *specifically military purposes* are excluded. Note that this still leaves the greater part of procurement by defence agencies within the terms of the directive, as much of their purchasing is not for specifically military purposes.

5. The procurement of supplies which are classified as '*secret*' or the delivery of supplies which involves *special security measures* are not within the scope of the directives.

Avoidance

Contracts cannot be split into separate parts to enable them to fall below the minimum value at which they must be advertised. The value placed on the contract must be related to a realistic, commercially determined valuation. Valuation principles are stated in the directive and should be studied closely. These principles include methods of valuing contracts financed by leasing or other methods.

Details to be given

The advertisement in the OJ must contain a range of information which will give a potential supplier enough detail to decide whether to make further enquiries and how to submit a bid. A copy of the Model Tender Notices is included as Appendix 3. The tender notice is published in full in the OJ in the language of the country of origin. A summary, only, is published in the other languages.

Advance information

From the beginning of 1989, large central government purchasing agencies (defined as those to whom the GATT rules apply) have been required to announce in advance their procurement plans in any product area where they are expected to exceed 750,000 ecu (£526,500) in their financial year. The Council was due to decide during 1990 whether to extend this requirement to all other public purchasing.

Retrospective information

The new rules require public authorities to report retrospectively the outcome of awards made by these procedures. These will be published in the OJ but will not include details which would harm the commercial interests of a firm. The price or range of price is a required item for publication but there is a dispensation (Article 9 of 88/295/EEC) allowing legitimate commercial interests to be introduced as justification for not doing so.

Tendering procedures

Open

Open tendering is the preferred method. Other methods can only be used when they can be specifically justified under the criteria laid down in the directives.

Selective

Selective (or *restricted* in the terms of the directive) tendering must be justified. Such justification may be accepted if the value of the contract does not merit the costs of open tender procedures or if the product is highly specific. Selective tendering will be monitored by the Commission through the submission by member states of a report on all selective tenders which justify the procedure, giving the value of the contract, the products purchased and the quantity, and the number of suppliers at each stage in the process. This information must be communicated to the Commission if the Commission so requests.

Negotiated

Negotiated (or single) tendering is permitted only in very closely defined circumstances. In abbreviated form, these are in cases:

- Where no suitable supplier was found in a previous open or restricted tender

- Where no bids at all were received in response to a previous tender

- Where the product is manufactured on a limited scale purely for the purposes of research

- Where there is, for technical or artistic reasons, only one available supplier in the Community

- Where extreme urgency results from unforeseen circumstances

- Where an original supplier is providing additional deliveries within a contract that usually does not exceed three years, and provided this was envisaged in the original contract document

Each of these conditions is stated here in an abbreviated form. Close reading of the fuller statements is absolutely essential if a claim for negotiated tendering is at issue.

Where negotiated tenders are awarded, the same reporting mechanism is imposed on the purchasing authority as is applied to selective tendering.

Time limits and intervals

Open tenders For open tenders the closing date will be at least fifty-two days after the notice is sent to the OJ. A subsidiary requirement is that the purchasing authority is obliged to supply tender documents within four working days of receiving a request from a potential bidder and is also obliged to supply requested supplementary information not later than six days before the closing date.

Selective tenders For selective tenders the closing date for applications to bid will be at least thirty-seven days after the notice is sent to the OJ. The minimum period to be allowed between the sending out of invitations to bid and the closing date for bids is 40 days.

Urgent cases Where the purchaser can prove the need for urgency, there is room to reduce these periods. This is an area of concern to many potential suppliers, although the Commission has indicated that any such exceptions should be rare (see Chapter 5).

Specifications

Purchasing authorities are now obliged to define technical specifications using national standards implementing European standards or by using 'common technical specifications', where these exist. In their absence, the principles of mutual recognition or equivalence should be used. This may be achieved by referring to national standards which implement international standards. Departure from these European standards is only merited where conformity testing is not possible, where products would be incompatible with existing equipment or there would be disproportionate costs or technical difficulties, or where the project is innovative. More detailed discussion on the use of common technical standards is contained in Part II of this book.

Disqualification

A potential supplier may be disqualified in defined circumstances. These include:

- Bankruptcy, or where the potential supplier is subject to bankruptcy proceedings

- Conviction of an offence in the potential supplier's professional conduct

- Grave professional misconduct

- Unfulfilled social security or tax payment obligations

- Serious misrepresentation of relevant details

Award criteria

At the preliminary stages of consideration of a bid, the purchaser may check the financial standing and technical competence of the organisation making a bid. The evidence which the purchaser may require in order to do this must be stated in the official tender notice. Suppliers may be required to show that they are on an official register of businesses in their home country.

The purchaser is allowed to use one of two criteria. These are either to award the contract to the tender offering the 'lowest price' or to award it to the 'most economically advantageous tender'. The second of these is obviously more subjective and is there to allow the purchaser to accept a tender which is *not* the lowest price, where other (non-cost) factors are important. The Directive lists examples of

Non price factors factors which may be taken into consideration. These include (besides price) delivery dates, running costs, cost effectiveness, quality, aesthetic and functional characteristics and after-sales service. The overriding principle that lies behind this guidance is that the criteria should be as objective as possible, should be capable of even application to all the bids, and that the criteria to be applied should be stated in advance in the contract documents or in the contract notice.

The debate among suppliers and potential suppliers on this topic centres on the room for abuse of non-price factors in arriving at a decision of the 'most economically advantageous tender'. Will this be used by purchasers to protect national champions or favoured suppliers? The Commission says not – the suppliers and potential suppliers say time will tell.

Effectiveness and enforcement

This list of rules for supplies contracts is wide-ranging and, stated in this form, may appear complex. However, the rules do provide an EC-wide code of practice which will, in theory, ensure that cross-border contracting is more likely to be determined by commercially justified criteria and to the benefit of the public sector customers.

At the time of writing, the new Directive has been in force for just over a year, so it is too early to assess whether it will be more effective than the earlier measures. The rules do, however, address the observed weaknesses in the former regime.

Later sections will turn to the legal issues which have so far been tested and to the wide debate still taking place on methods of enforcing the new rules.

4. How the system works – public works procedures

For building and civil engineering contracts, the public sector procedures in the EC are governed by two main directives. The first, approved in 1971, is 71/305/EEC. Formal approval for the second was given at the Council meeting on 18 July 1989 and was brought into force on 18 July 1990. The provisions of the new directive were published in July 1989 as 89/440/EEC.

These directives outline the procedures to be used which allow for, and encourage, the opening of the cross-border market to allow bids to be submitted by contractors throughout the EC.

The EC legislation should be regarded as a necessary supplement to, and not a substitute for, knowledge of the national, local or public sector enterprise in the target market and information on the procurement procedures that apply in each situation. National and local information will be obtained from diverse sources. Contractors will need to obtain information on the relevant market, the main clients and the competitor firms who already have local knowledge as an advantage.

For the five member states included in the Atkins study (Belgium, France, West Germany, Italy and the UK) there is information on their individual institutional structures (Part A, pp. 92–177). Further details on the national procedures for these five member states and the value of contracts paid for by the different agencies in 1984 are also provided in the study (Part A, pp. 178–309).

The requirements of the EC are designed to help all potential contractors to have better information and procedural reassurances on fairness. The full procedures will soon be in force for nine of the member states. In Greece, Spain and Portugal, the directives will become effective in 1992.

The rules

The following paragraphs give a broad summary of the EC rules which apply to public works tenders. A list of information sources for more details is to be found in Appendix 9. It is essential that tenders are correct and complete down to the smallest details and if in doubt appropriate professional advice should always be sought.

Advertising

Public works contracts must be advertised in the OJ. The information in the OJ is also made available through the Tenders Electronic Daily (TED) database. Further information on this database is given in Chapter 7.

Contract authorities

A public works contract may be defined as 'a contract for pecuniary consideration concluded in writing between a contractor and a contracting authority'. The contract includes the supply of equipment and materials. Contracts are defined so that the directives also include public works concession contracts. Broadly, the authorities include all government departments, local government, and publicly controlled education, health, police and housing bodies.

The concept of a public sector contract also extends to any project which is directly subsidised by more than 50 per cent from a public authority.

Exclusions

There are five general categories of excluded contracts:

1. At present, public trading utilities in *water*, *energy* and *transport* (but not ports and airports if the operators are public authorities or if, under the new Works Directive, a contract is 50 per cent funded by one) are still outside the scope of the directives.

2. *Small contracts* are excluded. These are less likely to be of interest on a cross-border basis and their exclusion removes a large amount of information from the system which would only infrequently be of value to external contractors. The limit set for small contracts in

1988 was 1 million ecu (approximately £662,000). The new directive has raised this lower limit to 5 million ecu (net of VAT) from 18 July 1990 (approximated to £3.31 million). This lower limit will be updated every two years to allow for the variance in conversion from ecu to national currencies.

When a possible contract is being valued to assess whether it must be advertised in the OJ and the EC procedures need to be applied, the value is related to the whole project regardless of whether it may be awarded in parts to different contractors or sub-contractors. Each part of the project which is likely to exceed 1 million ecu must be advertised. Parts of the contract awarded separately which do not exceed 1 million ecu may be excluded, subject to the provision that these smaller parts may not exceed 20 per cent of the value of the whole project.

Projects where a consortium is formed to bid for a whole project are treated as if the consortium was one firm bidding for a single contract.

3. Contracts linked to *awards made under international agreements* between an EC member state and a non-EC country where there is a joint project (possibly related to development aid) is excluded as are contracts for certain international agencies.

4. Contracts for *specifically military purposes* are excluded. Note that this still leaves the greater part of procurement by defence agencies within the terms of the directive, as much of their purchasing is not for specifically military purposes.

5. Works contracts which are classified as '*secret*' or the execution of which involves *special security measures* are not within the scope of the directives.

Avoidance

Contracts cannot be split into separate parts to enable them to fall below the minimum value at which they must be advertised. The value placed on the contract must be related to a realistic, commercially determined valuation. Valuation principles are stated in the directive and should be studied closely. These include methods of valuing contracts financed by leasing or by other methods.

Details to be given

The advertisement in the OJ must contain a range of information which will give a potential contractor enough detail to decide whether to make further enquiries and how to submit a bid. A copy of the Model Tender Notices is included as Appendix 3. The tender notice is published in full in the OJ in the language of the country of origin. A summary, only, is published in the other languages.

In order to assist potential sub-division of the contract, authorities may divide the contract into lots and invite bids for one, several, or all the parts, subject to the rules stated above.

Advance information

The most recent directive asks the public authorities to publish an indicative notice which gives an outline of major public works contracts which may be awarded in the next year. This is to alert possible tenderers to the situation and may assist them in organising their business priorities. The notice is to include details of the organisation likely to be seeking bids, the site of the contract, the services to be provided and, if available, an estimate of the cost of the contract. Also recommended for inclusion is information on the dates expected for the award of the contract, the likely start date and the timetable for completion of the work, as well as an indication of the financing arrangements envisaged.

Retrospective information

The new rules require public authorities to report retrospectively the outcome of awards made by these procedures. These will be published in the OJ but will not include details which would harm the commercial interests of either the firm to whom the contract was awarded or of the public authority. The required details include the name of the successful contractor, the price, or range of prices paid, the number of offers received for the contract, the date the award was made, the procedure chosen in the decision making and the criteria used for the award. This information is to be sent to the Commission within forty-eight days of the awarding of the contract.

Tenderers, or eliminated candidates, may ask why they have been unsuccessful and the name of the successful tenderer. The public authority awarding the contract must provide this information within fifteen days of the request being received. If no award is made, the authority is obliged to inform the unsuccessful firms of the reason why no award was made.

Tendering procedures

Open

Open tendering is favoured, but other methods can be used when justified under the criteria laid down in the directives.

Selective

Selective (or restricted) tendering must be justified. The usual reason for the use of this method is to allow the public authority to deal with a group of possible tenderers who are assessed at a preliminary stage for their competence in the type of work under offer. This procedure must allow firms across the Community an opportunity to be considered on an objective basis alongside their competitors. The public authority awarding the contract under this procedure may indicate the number of firms or the range within which it intends to invite to tender. It is expected, if practical, to be at least five and may be up to twenty.

Negotiated

Negotiated tendering is permitted only in very closely defined circumstances. The number of firms considered in negotiations may not be less than three, provided there are sufficient applicants. In abbreviated form, the use of negotiated tendering is acceptable when, after earlier publication of a tender invitation and the identification of candidates who meet certain basic criteria:

- The tenders were irregular or unacceptable

- The works are only for research purposes

- The nature of the works or the risks involved do not permit the overall fixing of a price in advance

or without earlier publication of a tender invitation when:

- No suitable supplier was found in a previous open or restricted tender

- No bids at all were received in response to a previous tender

- There is, for technical or artistic reasons, or for the protection of exclusive rights, only one appropriate contractor

- Extreme urgency results from unforeseen circumstances

- Additional works not in the original contract arise through unforeseen circumstances, which cannot be separated from the main contract without great inconvenience, or are strictly necessary to the later stages. Additional works may not exceed 50 per cent of the amount of the main contract.

- It is a repetition of similar works undertaken in an earlier contract, provided that notice of the possible repeat contracts was given in the original tender notice and their value was taken into account in deciding if the works were to be advertised (i.e. exceeded 5 million ecu in total – see page 29).

In the 1971 Directive, Article 9 provided for non-competitive tendering as an exception but is regarded as having allowed too great a degree of discretion for public authorities (until recently a large percentage of contracts, possibly as high as 25 per cent, were being awarded using this justification). The 1989 Directive has repealed this article and tightened the conditions for negotiated tendering.

Where negotiated tenders are awarded a formal report on the reasons and the outcome has to be drawn up and sent to the Commission if it so requests.

Time limits and intervals

Open tenders For open tenders the closing date will be at least fifty-two days after the notice is sent to the OJ. Where an advance indication of the works contract has already been published in the OJ (see page 31) then this time period may be reduced to 36 days. A subsidiary requirement is that the public authority is obliged to supply tender documents within six days of receiving a request from a potential bidder and is also obliged to supply requested supplementary information not later than six days before the closing date. If these time limits cannot be observed, where documents or other materials cannot be supplied in time, or if site visits are an essential part of the preparation of a bid, then the time limits must be extended appropriately.

Selective tenders For selective tenders, using the restricted or negotiated procedures, the closing date for applications to bid will be at least 37 days after the notice is sent to the OJ. This is reduced to 26 where there has been a sufficiently detailed earlier indicative notice of the intention to seek tenders. When the restricted procedure is used, the minimum period to be allowed between the sending out of invitations to bid and the closing date for bids will be 40 days.

Urgent cases Where the public authority can prove the need for urgency, there is room to reduce these periods. This is an area of concern to many potential suppliers (see Chapter 5).

Specifications

Contract awarding authorities are now obliged to define technical specifications using national standards implementing European standards or by using 'common technical specifications', where these exist. In their absence, the principles of mutual recognition or equivalence may be used. This may be achieved by referring to national standards which implement international standards, other national standards or technical approvals. Departure from these guidelines is only merited where no guidelines can be obtained, where products would be incompatible with existing equipment or there would be disproportionate costs or technical difficulties, or where the project is innovative. More detailed discussion on the use of common technical standards is contained in Part II of this book.

Disqualification

A potential contractor may be disqualified in defined circumstances. These include:

- Bankruptcy, or where the potential supplier is subject to bankruptcy proceedings

- Conviction of an offence in the potential supplier's professional conduct

- Grave professional misconduct

- Unfulfilled social security or tax payment obligations

- Serious misrepresentation of relevant details

Award criteria

At the preliminary stages of consideration of a bid, the contractors can be asked to demonstrate their financial standing and technical competence. The evidence which may be required by the purchaser must be stated in the official tender notice. Contractors may be required to show that they are on an official register of businesses in their home country.

The contract may be awarded using one of two criteria. These are either to award the contract to the tender offering the 'lowest price' or to award it to the 'most economically advantageous tender'. The second of these is obviously more subjective and is there to allow the purchaser to accept a tender which is not the lowest price, where other (non-cost) factors are important. The directive lists examples of factors which may be taken into consideration. These include (besides price), period for completion, running costs, profitability, technical merit, etc. The new directive allows that consideration can also be given to variations in the tender as long as it meets the minimum specifications, provided this possibility is acknowledged in the official tender notice. The over-riding principle that lies behind this guidance is that the criteria should be as objective as possible, and should be capable of even application to all the bids.

When making an award, the public authority is allowed to introduce a contractual condition that links the contract with job creation. The condition is to be contained in the tender notice (see the reference to case 31/87, the Beentjes case, in Appendix 1) and must be non-discriminatory.

Effectiveness and enforcement

This list of rules for works contracts is wide-ranging and, stated in this form, may appear complex. However, the rules do provide an EC-wide code of practice which should ensure that cross-border contracting is more likely to be determined by commercially justified criteria and to the benefit of the public sector customers.

At the time of writing, the new directive has not yet come into force, so it is too early to assess how much more effective than the earlier measures it will be. The rules do, however, address the observed weaknesses in the former regime.

Later sections will turn to the legal issues which have so far been tested and to the wide debate still taking place on methods of enforcing the new rules.

5. Enforcing the rules

Directives on public procurement have developed faster than policies to ensure that they are enforced. Since the 1992 programme was launched in 1985, there has been an acknowledgement that enforcement mechanisms were insufficiently rigorous and varied unacceptably from one member state to another.

There may have been an expectation that, since the directives had to be implemented by national governments and other public authorities, specific EC-based enforcement measures would not be necessary. Public sector agencies might be expected to observe rules made by their own government procedures. Governments would be keen to see both spirit and letter of the directives enforced. Whatever the expectation, there appear to be a large number of failures to publish tender notices in the OJ. This has created a suspicion that some awards of contracts have been made which could have been challenged, had there been knowledge of them.

The current enforcement mechanisms

The situation as it stands in mid 1990 allows for the use of enforcement mechanisms, or an application for redress, to be considered in two ways. First, aggrieved potential suppliers can use their national **National** administrative arrangements or courts to consider their rights under **arrangements** Community law, as defined by the EC Treaties or by national legislation implementing Community directives where they exist. The strength of these mechanisms varies from country to country in scope, remedies, and timing. Second, the Commission itself can receive a complaint from an aggrieved supplier, or a third party such as the government of another member state, and after investigation the complaint may be adjudicated by the European Court of Justice. Examples of some of the cases heard by the Court are summarised in Appendix 1.

There are weaknesses in both these options. The Commission would prefer to create a stronger and more equitable enforcement mechanism to be applied by each member state. The Commission does not wish to place a greater reliance on the European Court. This is in the interests of efficiency in dealing with complaints and seeking speedy decisions, as well as allowing the European Court to function more as a court of appeal.

The Commission's wish list

In the practical enforcement of the rules on public procurement the Commission identified specific remedies that it would have wished to see made available in each member state. These included:

- A means of securing speedy action, including interim measures, where possible

- The ability to have an award suspended while it is investigated

- The ability to have a decision set aside

- The possibility of damages for an aggrieved supplier

- The admission of a complaint from a third party, such as the Commission

Diversity of arrangements

In a working paper published in December 1988, the Commission compared the position on remedies in the field of public procurement in each of the member states. The comparison illustrated the variety of institutional arrangements and also the differences in the nature of the remedies which could be sought. It illustrated by the degree of diversity in both, why the Commission was concerned to gain agreement to a further directive which would create certain minimum remedial powers through the administrative or judicial institutions in each member state.

In Annex 1 to the working paper, the Commission gives the following examples of differences between national systems:

'As regards administrative appeals:

- These are usually organised on a purely practical basis, which does not provide the complainant with any real safeguards; some member states (France, Greece, Italy, Portugal and Spain) do have a relatively well-structured system of administrative appeal, however;

- Suspension of an award decision is recognised in only a few member states;

- It is not possible in all member states to set aside or withdraw an award decision;

- It is virtually impossible anywhere in the Community for injured firms to obtain damages direct from the administrative authorities.

'As regards appeals to the courts:

- In some member states, suspension of an award decision is recognised only exceptionally and is virtually never granted in practice;

- In certain member states, it is not possible for an award decision to be set aside;

- The possibility of obtaining damages is subject in certain member states to limits and uncertainties such that it is largely theoretical;

- The possibility of intervention by third parties in an appeal to the courts also varies considerably; in some member states it does not exist.'

The proposed enforcement measures

In July 1987 the Commission prepared a draft directive which was designed to ensure that member states introduced certain common standards and rules on the remedies which they would offer when redress was sought (and justified) in the application of the rules for the award of public sector contracts. An amended draft was published in January 1989 taking account of amendments arising from the recommendations of the European Parliament.

The broad thrust of the proposals was that enforcement, and the application of remedies, would largely be administered within individual member states. The particular institutional arrangements would vary between states. The current law of member states would be applied to disputed contracts subject to the provisions of the directive.

After discussion at the Council, and debate at the Parliament, a directive was adopted formally on 21 December 1989. The Directive places on member states an obligation to:

- Introduce effective and rapid remedies

- Include provision for 'interim' measures, including the suspension of contract award procedures (but not necessarily the power to suspend a contract, once let)

- Allow the possibility of making an order to remove discriminatory provisions and award damages to firms adversely affected (but not necessarily including damages for loss of profits)

- Reply within 21 days to a request from the Commission to correct what it considers to be 'clear and manifest infringement'

Enforcement Directive

In contrast to the present complaints procedure available to the Commission (through Article 169 of the Treaty), the proposed powers should give a more effective and quicker answer in most cases. The new Enforcement Directive is one of the fundamental components of the 1992 programme being urged by the Commission and needs to be brought into force in each member state by 1 December 1991. In the interim period, aggrieved suppliers and contractors will continue to rely on a combination of very differing sets of national law and administration and on the somewhat slow and cumbersome mechanisms of a direct complaint to the Commission.

The main revisions to the Directive as originally drafted reduce the proposed direct influence of the Commission on the legal processes in member states and leave this responsibility with national authorities. The logic is clear. Governments have the responsibility for enforcing directives. However there must be a worry that, despite the legal logic, businesses in the UK interested in non-UK markets might be more reassured of enforcement of the Directive if more of the initiative lay with the Commission.

The Commission emphasises that 'any firm is free to complain directly to the Commission'. This can be done in writing to either a local Euro-Info Centre or to the Directorate-General for the Internal Market and Industrial Affairs (200 rue de la Loi, B-1049 Brussels). Complaints should be made quickly so that the chance to secure corrective action is not missed simply because of delay or because events have progressed to a point where remedies are more complex.

6. Broadening the scope: The pressure to extend the provisions

Excluded sectors

The Commission published late in 1988, proposals to extend the public procurement principles to the main enterprises which are owned, controlled or regulated by governments. Such enterprises are identified by taking account of the degree to which they operate in a normal competitive market, are insulated from market forces, and are exposed to influence or regulation by the government.

These three principles are determined by such features as the existence of a natural monopoly (water mains, electricity grids, etc.) or the provision of services in a defined geographical area (e.g. coal or oil exploration, or the provision of an airport).

These public sector trading enterprises are often referred to as the utilities or excluded sectors (excluded, that is, from the procedures introduced in the 1970s for central and local government and other public authorities).

The scale of the purchases by public sector enterprises which are not subject to the existing rules, is considerable. The Atkins study found that for the five member states in their survey, public sector enterprises accounted for 41 per cent of all public purchasing. This represents an annual spending total of nearly 200 billion ecu for the whole EC.

Service contracts

A further extension of public procurement policies to cover service contracts has also been suggested and is discussed more fully below.

The public sector trading enterprises

Two draft directives were published late in 1988, but after discussions with the European Parliament and the Economic and Social Committee, the Commission (in July 1989) consolidated these into one proposal on which a common position (i.e. an agreement in principle) was reached on 29 March 1990. The directive deals with entities which provide water, energy and transport services and certain 'network' parts of the telecommunications sector. The intention is that the directive will apply to businesses in these sectors whether they are publicly or privately owned. A list of the organisations to be included has been published, although it is not definitive. In other words, omission from the list does not exempt a purchaser from the proposed regulations if the purchaser still meets the criteria. The list is sub-divided into those enterprises engaged in:

- Drinking-water (production, transport or distribution)

- Electricity (production, transport or distribution). Independent electricity producers are excluded under defined conditions, if they are not linked for significant sales to the national grid. Purchases of energy and fuel by energy producers are to be excluded, at present.

- Gas or heat (production, transport or distribution)

- Oil and gas (exploration for and extraction, but excluding the refining and distribution of oil)

- Coal and solid fuels (exploration for and extraction of)

- Railway services

- Urban railways, tramways, trolley bus, cable or bus services (but excluding bus transport services that do not enjoy any degree of market protection)

- Airport terminal facilities

- Maritime and inland port or other terminal facilities

- Provision or operation of a public telecommunications network or provision of telecommunications services

As a general rule, where an enterprise has other business activities outside the main identified areas listed above, those other activities are not subject to the proposed regulations

The following sectors are not within the scope of the new legislation:

- Road haulage
- Private coach services
- Transport services by sea
- Inland waterway services
- Airlines
- Refining, transport and distribution of petroleum goods
- Sea ferry services

(Operators of small inshore or river ferries will be brought within the scope of the Works and Supplies Directive if their activities are carried on essentially for reasons of public or social service and not as a commercial activity.)

Telecommunications

The position regarding telecommunications is complicated. The pattern of ownership of telecommunications services varies between the member states: some are state owned; others are private companies. The principle which the Commission is trying to follow is that equipment which is linked to the 'reserved' or monopoly type services should be subject to procurement rules, since in these areas there is a tendency for national firms to gain a preferential relationship. In non-protected services, normal competition makes this approach unnecessary. Excluded from the proposed procurement rules are, therefore:

- Terminal equipment
- Telecommunications services, other than those protected by special or exclusive rights (which at present includes the main network infrastructure and the voice telephone services)
- The purchase of equipment for resale or hire

The draft directive will, therefore, apply to the transmission and switching equipment which enables use of public and private terminals.

Method of application to the excluded sectors

Contracts on offer from all the firms covered by the above definitions must be made available to potential suppliers inside and outside the individual member state. The decision to award the contract must be made on non-discriminatory objective criteria. However, the purchasing enterprises will be given more flexibility in the methods which they are permitted to use than apply to public authorities. The choice between open, restricted or negotiated procedures will be more flexible, and will lie with the purchasing enterprise. This allows close and continuing links between certain firms and their suppliers.

Negotiated procedures cannot be used without a prior call for potential suppliers to indicate an interest (one exception being when the purchasing enterprises claim overwhelming urgency). Potential suppliers would have a right to know the criteria to qualify for consideration, the selection criteria and the criteria determining the award, in advance of making a bid. If a supplier is disappointed, the result of the award could normally be made available to them. There is a requirement to publish a periodic notice in the OJ inviting potential suppliers to express an interest.

The same minimum value exclusion clauses would apply as for works (5 million ecu) but for supplies the thresholds are 0.4 million ecu other than for telecommunications where the threshold will be 0.6 million ecu.

The remainder of the Directive sets similar procedures for the award of contracts as already exist in the Works and Supplies Directives. Indeed, this similarity is regarded as too close by many of the enterprises who would like to have an even more flexible framework. Discussion has centred on the proposed requirement for regular 'periodic indicative notices', time constraints on open or restricted tendering, requirements to supply operating specifications to potential suppliers, and record keeping for potential requests for information from the Commission. All of these proposed requirements are regarded as burdensome for enterprises which in many cases operate commercially.

Public procurement of services

The purchasing of services by the public sector is the latest area to receive attention from the Commission. The proposal will be for a directive to apply to all bodies covered by the Works and Supplies Directives. A further proposal is expected later on the procurement of services by the utilities.

The advisory committee for the opening of public procurement has received a number of discussion papers, in which services are defined so that all public sector procurement would be either works, or supplies, or services, or an 'exceptional category' (which might include, for example, all contracts for the purchase, lease or renting of land and buildings).

The in-house provision of services would be excluded. So also would those services which are reserved (by legislation or other official regulatory mechanism, for example) to particular public authorities (special agencies which are established to monitor safety or standards would fall into this category). The intention is to include only those services which are supplied through some type of market mechanism. Services related to defence, state security and international agreements would be excluded.

Services which the Commission propose should be subject to the full application of a new directive include:

- Architecture
- Engineering and other construction-related services (including testing, surveying, design, and consultancy)
- Computers and related services
- Management consultancy
- Sewage and refuse disposal
- Professional consultancy in various fields of expertise
- Transport services
- Printing and publication
- Telecommunications services
- Advertising
- Building cleaning

Less easily included, and therefore subject to a less rigorous application of procurement rules, would be:

- Hotel and restaurant services
- Research and development services (R&D)
- Legal services
- Health and social services
- Recreational services

The Commission is considering whether it should approach definition by specifying particular activities or by making general statements into which activities would fall. For example, 'service contracts which have as their object activities of an industrial or commercial character' would include software, management consultancy, maintenance and cleaning, etc. A similar general statement might be aimed at professional services.

The discussion document allows that there are other services which would not be a priority for inclusion in new requirements. These might be asked to observe only some basic formalities such as advertising the outcome of contracts awarded. Firmer proposals are expected later in 1990.

What now, and when?

As will be apparent, these discussions are at an early stage. No final decisions should be expected until 1991–2, although representative bodies should be considering their reaction and lobbying now.

7.   Sources of information

To realise the potential benefits from the opening up of the internal market for public procurement, businesses must not only have the right to bid across boundaries, they must also have information about the opportunities. The Commission must enforce the rights *and* ensure that opportunities are widely publicised.

In a perfect system, all public procurement contracts which exceed the minimum stipulated values, will be advertised in the OJ. Potential suppliers will then respond using the different approved types of procedure. Whether the advertising of notices in this way will be adequate remains to be seen. Few contracts will rely solely on the Commission publication. No Commission action is a substitute for your own market assessment. Commission actions try to make the access for a British firm to the market in other member states, as easy as the access of a firm in Bradford to the opportunities in Edinburgh. Most businesses which have an interest in increasing their activity in a member state other than their home state will undertake some preparatory investigation.

Accessing the information

Official Journal

The basic Commission source of information is the OJ. The new Works and Supplies Directives and the expected strengthening of the enforcement mechanisms, will serve to increase the amount of information available on each contract and the assurance that it will be published. The usual contract notice will be summarised in each main EC language and a fuller statement (of up to 650 words) will be published in the language of the contract. This limit does not apply in the Common Position on Utilities Directive, although it is in the Supplies and Works Directive as amended. Further information will be supplied to enquirers.

The Commission has made the notices available through a database which is updated daily. Tenders Electronic Daily, often abbreviated **TED** to TED, is an online source of the information in the OJ. TED also includes notices for contracts in the African, Caribbean and Pacific countries linked to the EC, partly because of the requirements when they use development funds from the EC, as well as a number of Japanese contracts. Further discussions are currently taking place to consider the addition of contract notices from EFTA, Canada and the USA. Contracts coming under the GATT code are also published here. Since early in 1989, TED has also been used to publish the names of companies which have been awarded contracts.

The number of official contract notices will exceed 20,000 each year. You will usually only be interested in a small percentage of these. TED can be used selectively. Tender notices are classified according to the four-digit NACE code used for industrial classifications in the EC. A user can, therefore, define a request for information by the type of product and the country originating the notice.

These services involve a user charge as well as the need for a basic modem and terminal, or telex machine. The cost entails both the telephone time and the cost of access to the database.

The TED database and others are operated by the European Communities Host Organisation (ECHO) and the address for reference is:

ECHO Customer Service
BP 2373
L-1023 Luxembourg
Luxembourg GD
(Tel: 010–352 488041)

Supplementary sources

Businesses which wish to make other enquiries about public procurement in member states may wish to approach the originating agencies direct. There is no complete or standard reference for this purpose. However a list of relevant agencies is given in the annexes to the GATT Agreement on Government Procurement, as an annex to the Supplies Directive, as Appendices 1 and 2 to the European Documentation pamphlet 'Public procurement and construction; towards an integrated market', and as annexes to the draft directive for the excluded sectors.

Wider dimensions

Sub-contracting

Greater knowledge of contract opportunities, and increased knowledge of the outcome of award procedures, opens up a new and extensive source of information of potential value to sub-contractors and subsidiary suppliers. The name and location of a successful main contractor is a useful starting point for many small sub-contractors. So also is the procedure which asks works contracts to identify the probable areas and amounts of sub-contracting when a tender notice is published.

A recent development which will facilitate this process is the publication through TED of the names of companies which have been awarded contracts. This will help sub-contractors take advantage of the opening of the market to the larger main contractors or suppliers.

Structural Funds

All contracts funded from Structural Funds (Regional, Social and Agricultural Guarantee Funds, for example) and the European Investment Bank must observe the public procurement regulations. This means that the details of the allocation of such funds should be watched carefully – they provide an indication of likely sources of major contracts.

II
Technical barriers to trade

8. Technical barriers and their effect

What is a technical barrier to trade? It is created by the disparities between national technical regulations and standards. These compel manufacturers either to restrict themselves to one (usually, their own) national market, or to invest in costly research and adaptation of their product to comply with the technical regulations and standards in a new market into which they wish to sell. Such barriers to trade are by their very nature varied and complex. One definition explains it in this way: 'If a producer who wishes to sell his products or services in another Community country has to modify them to comply with industrial standards or with national regulations, or has to subject them to additional testing or certification procedures, he faces a technical barrier to trade.'

Forms of technical barriers to trade

There are three main types of technical barriers to trade.

Differences in national standards

These are based on custom, practice and procedure. National standards are not legal requirements but are established by consensus among industries. They are reinforced in some member states by the policies and practices of insurance companies. We are all familiar with British Standards, BS numbers and the kite mark; many manufacturers know of DIN, the German national standards authority.

The most important aspect of standards is their voluntary nature. They are drawn up by agreement between manufacturers, purchasers, consumers and others with an interest in common standards. They are thus created by industry to serve its commercial needs. No standards authority has the power to force compliance with national, European or international standards, they are 'enforced' only by commercial and market realities (and equally can be overtaken by changes in the market). In spite of not being legally binding, they may assume quasi-legal status because they are often referred to in technical regulations as a means of demonstrating compliance for product liability claims and insurance purposes.

Differences in national regulations

National regulations are similar to standards in their impact but *are* legally binding and are established to protect the public interest – health, safety and the environment. National regulations have also been used to protect local industries, especially in the food products sector.

Testing and certification requirements

The usual method of ensuring conformity to national standards is by testing or certification. A technical barrier to trade is imposed every time a member state requires testing or certification *additional* to that required in the country of origin. Testing and certification requirements can, in practice, be the most onerous form of technical barrier to trade, and can add significantly to the cost of goods. It is essential to remember that much testing and certification is carried out to meet the needs of customers for market information, and may continue even in a more integrated market. A typical problem is the non-recognition by one member state of the certification process of another, meaning at best additional testing and at worst an absolute market barrier. Because of the nature of the problem, a different market approach is needed in tackling trade barriers from dissimilar national testing and certification arrangements.

Each of these forms of technical barrier has subtly different effects on industry. Taken together they have a substantial deterrent effect on trade and would, if allowed to remain, be an increasing drag on the dynamism of the 1992 programme. It is easy to see why. In an increasing number of sectors, firms will be obliged to survive by selling much larger quantities than are likely to be absorbed by their immediate national market. To compete they will have to produce on a greater scale, which will involve new investment in research and innovation. National product regulations have a quite contradictory logic, however, because they reinforce production oriented towards the national market. Both alternatives – to limit oneself to a sub-optimal market or to attack new markets via new specific technology – imply extensive costs.

The effect of technical barriers

It is useful to take the three forms of barriers to trade in turn and examine to what degree they impact on businesses in the Community.

National regulations

Achieving the free movement of goods in the Community is central to the drive to create a single market. That objective has been frustrated by the differences in national regulations arising from obligations that all member states impose on business for reasons of public- or self-interest. Differences in national regulations also create barriers to trade.

Some of the differences in national regulations relate to issues such as consumer protection and public health, others reflect different approaches to achieving the same effect and yet others relate to a wish to protect particular interest groups or industries. In Denmark, for example, beer bottles are required to be returnable and – possibly as a result – beer imports to the Danish market account for less than 0.1 per cent of consumption. Italian legislation formerly required that pasta be made of durum wheat. Pasta produced in other member states (which have no such requirement) could not be sold in Italy if it was not made from durum wheat. That regulation has now been changed, but others will be more difficult to get round (for example, the requirement in the UK and the Republic of Ireland that cars are manufactured to be driven on the left).

Regulatory differences have a particular impact on the food and drink industries where special legislation to protect public health exists in every country.

National standards

Differences in standards limit the ability of European industry to enter, sell to and invest in other member states. For example, in the construction industry there are different national standards in Germany (DIN), France (AFNOR) and Britain (BSI). In the past, each national standards authority in the Community has made its own standards reflecting its own traditions and the needs of its industry.

Standards have no binding legal force (although they may be referred to in legislation) but they *are* used in contracts and are the basis of national custom and practice. In the construction industry, for example, insurance companies may be unwilling to make a payment unless the appropriate national standard has been met. In many cases architects are inclined to use standards to limit exposure to damages suits. In West Germany, conformity to a standard is a defence against legal action for damages resulting from an alleged product defect.

However, a standard is only relevant to the extent to which the market continues to recognise and use it. If a standard is introduced which flies in the face of the demands of the market, then products which do not conform to the standard may well continue to sell. In time such a standard is likely to become obsolete or to be modified to suit the demands of the market.

Differences in standards and specifications tailored to national suppliers have a particular impact on sectors such as construction, heavy electrical products and telecommunictions (both exchange systems and consumer equipment). A particular example is the range of systems for car telephones now in use in Europe. The British system is incompatible with, at least, the Irish, French and Italian systems. (However, it should be noted that the Council of Ministers has now adopted a Directive and Resolution on mobile telephones within the Community which should, over time, have the effect of reducing such divergences).

Testing and certification

Producers, suppliers and users often want to be sure that a product conforms to a standard or a specification. This market requirement is met by testing, certification and inspection. Yet this can result in repeated testing of the same product across different markets at considerable extra cost. Where an attempt is being made to market across national barriers this will constitute a barrier to trade. Examples of industries particularly affected by differences in testing and certification procedures are the pharmaceutical industry, in which an individual drug is subject to repeated testing for the same information, and the automobile industry, which is subject to differing national type approvals.

9. The differential impact

A series of studies performed throughout the Community for the Commission examined 'the cost of non-Europe' as a result of various factors, including the impact of differences in standards and other technical requirements. One of these studies attempted to measure the views of industry to the different forms of barriers to the completion of the internal market. Two other studies were specifically related to technical barriers to trade.

In the survey of views of industry on the importance of the various obstacles to the completion of the internal market, technical barriers were regarded as the most important form of obstacle by industry in the UK, West Germany and France, and in the Community as a whole.

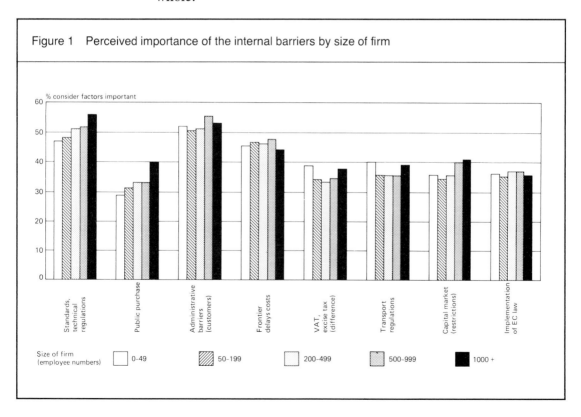

Figure 1   Perceived importance of the internal barriers by size of firm

Figure 1 shows the response of industry throughout the Community to these questions. The striking point is that it is the largest firms which find technical barriers to trade the major impediment to the completion of the internal market. This suggests that even the largest firms cannot overcome the effect of technical barriers merely by using additional human and financial resources. In other words, technical barriers to trade are the most obstinate form of barrier to the creation of the internal market.

In another study, carried out by the French consulting firm Groupe MAC, an attempt was made to put these findings of the various detailed studies into an overall context. Groupe MAC summarised its findings about the sectoral impact of different forms of technical barriers as shown in the following table:

Figure 2 The Groupe MAC study			
Industry	Types and incidences of technical barriers		
	Standards	Regulations	Authorisation
Foodstuffs	L	H	L
Pharmaceuticals	L	L	H
Automobiles	L	I	H
Building materials	H	I	H
Electrical products and machines High voltage Low voltage	H L	I L	H L
Telecommunications	H	L	H

H high incidence/impact on trade
I   intermediate incidence/impact on trade
L low/non-existent

The Groupe MAC diagram (Figure 2) illustrates the incidence of technical barriers to trade in six industrial sectors studied by Groupe MAC. It provides a framework for looking at the differential impact on sectors and of different types of requirements. At the general level there are four interesting points:

● Differences in standards, which are voluntary requirements, are of the greatest importance in the old industrial sectors which had developed independently of one another over a long period.

- Differences in national regulations have a particular impact in the sectors which directly affect human health and safety (e.g. foodstuffs and electrical safety).

- Authorisation and certification barriers have widespread effects and are likely to be very costly for an individual manufacturer to overcome.

- While high voltage electrical products suffer from all of the forms of barriers, low voltage products are free from barriers. This is an illustration of the benefit of European harmonisation – a low voltage electrical products directive was brought into force as early as 1973 and studies of the industry demonstrate the benefits which such harmonisation can provide.

The sectoral impact of technical barriers to trade

Outlined below is a brief analysis of the review carried out for the Commission on the impact of technical barriers to trade across six key sectors.

Food

The types of barrier impacting on particular sectors obviously vary considerably. In foodstuffs, given the extreme sensitivity of public opinion on the issue, standards are almost non-existent but regulations abound. The sensitivity of public opinion, the variety of culinary traditions in the Community and the degree of nationalism associated with particular dishes mean that regulations constitute a very significant barrier to trade in the footstuffs sector. Groupe MAC found over 200 technical trade barriers resulting from regulations in just ten food product sectors. Interestingly, technical barriers resulting from certification and testing requirements are not common in the food sector.

For the food industry regulations fall under three main headings:

1. *Product composition* laws relating to the use of a generic product name, (e.g. the use of a name such as pasta, beer, chocolate or ice-cream may be restricted to products which correspond to a particular recipe or contain particular ingredients)

2. *Specific ingredient restrictions.* Laws which prohibit or require the use of specific ingredients are a major cause of barriers to trade in

the food sector (for example, the requirement formerly for the use of durum wheat in Italian pasta and the prohibition formerly of the use of the sweetener aspartame in France). Very often the existence of such regulations is justified by member states on grounds of public safety or health and, under Article 36 of the Treaty of Rome, such situations are permitted, but very often the form of the restriction imposed has been found to benefit well established local producers' interests.

3. *Packaging and labelling laws.* Such laws are often justified on grounds of protection of human health or of the environment. A total of 150 Italian municipalities prohibit the sale of mineral water in plastic bottles because of the environmental pollution caused by the disposal of such bottles. The prohibition, however, creates a substantial market advantage for local bottlers. Similarly, Denmark, as we have seen, requires that beer be sold in returnable bottles. The expense involved in setting up a collection-on-return system by non-indigenous bottlers is very high and results in an extremely low level of penetration of the Danish beer market by foreign producers.

Pharmaceuticals

In the pharmaceutical sector specifications are upheld by national regulations. Eleven directives harmonise basic criteria such as quality, safety and efficacy but severe technical barriers remain due to the persistence of national certification and testing regimes. Often these national regimes have much to do with the importance of low drug prices to national public expenditure on health care.

Each EC member state requires a separate marketing authorisation procedure before a drug can be offered on its market. These procedures are supposed to be completed in 120 days but no member state can regularly meet this requirement at present. The average delay is of the order of 18 to 24 months for each national authorisation, and the process may have to be repeated by a large manufacturer in all twelve member states. Estimates of the costs of these barriers can be as high as 2 per cent of total industry costs in the sector.

Automobiles

In the automobile sector standards play a relatively minor role as a barrier to trade and the influence of regulations has been reduced by a series of EC harmonisation measures.

Although to date 41 out of 44 'essential requirements' have been harmonised across the Community, differences remain and there has been relatively little progress towards eliminating the remaining differences. This reluctance to complete the process has been attributed to the desire of some member states to prevent the opening up of European car markets to Far Eastern producers who were seen as likely to benefit most from being able to sell vehicles conforming to common standards throughout the Community. However, the reappointed Commission of January 1989 is taking a much more vigorous line on such issues and has announced plans for early progress on the completion of the harmonisation of the 'essential requirements' relating to automobiles.

Proposals on the three remaining areas were detailed in January 1990 (referring to weights and dimensions, tyres and windscreens). They have proved controversial in past discussions and an early agreement may not be achieved.

In the absence of complete harmonisation at the European level, national inspection arrangements constitute a real barrier to trade in the motor industry. The estimated savings from elimination of these barriers are of the order of £9–12 million per annum.

An indication of the extent of market fragmentation in this sector is the persistence of real differences in price levels for comparable models between member states, although prices are affected by a much wider range of factors than the standards issue, in particular national taxation regimes. Some illustrative figures are given in the table below.

WEST GERMAN CARS

Prices of comparable vehicles in European markets (1987)

Belgium	100
France	115
West Germany	127
Italy	129
UK	142

[Source: *European Economy* (March 1988)]

Anyone who has taken advantage of a personal import scheme for cars will know the scale of these distortions.

Building products

A study carried out for the European Commission found that 70 per cent of a sample of building material products suffered barriers in the form of standards or regulations, and that this was often reinforced by differences in testing and certification procedures.

Barriers to the use of foreign building products are deeply entrenched, in part because of history and tradition, in part because of climatic differences and in part to protect local production. It was found, for example, that Spanish roof tiles are about 50 per cent cheaper than French tiles but the market in France is effectively protected because (1) French workers are not familiar with the fixing method for the Spanish product, (2) a particularly stringent national standard is applied to public sector contracts and specified by architects and (3) products not meeting the standard must be certified on an annual basis and the process of certification can take up to twelve months to complete. A directive to harmonise the requirements which can be applied to construction products was agreed by the Council of Ministers in June 1988 and will come into force no later than 27 June 1991 (i.e. within 30 months of notification to the member states on 27 December 1988).

Electrical products

This sector falls into two parts, high voltage products and low voltage products. The former (mainly industrial products) suffer from all of the types of barriers to trade, including regulations relating to operator safety. By comparison, low voltage products are relatively free of restrictions because Community law relating to low voltage electrical products was harmonised in 1973. This Low Voltage Directive is in fact the precursor of and role model for the so-called 'new approach' directives which lie at the heart of the Commission's current work on harmonisation of technical requirements and which are discussed in Chapter 10.

Telecommunications

Product specifications in the telecommunications industry do not, by and large, directly affect public health or safety. Regulation has, therefore, been left largely to the industry itself. As a result barriers to trade in this industry generally take the form of standards and testing and certification procedures relating to those standards. The evidence suggests that the standards applied by the national postal and telecommunications authorities are excessively stringent, and that the testing procedures are slow, duplicative and costly. The reduction in product costs which would result if the barriers to the entry of telecommunications products to the West German market were removed are estimated at 3 per cent of present costs. The average delays in certification in various European markets are summarised below.

Telecommunications certification delays	
Member state	*Delay*
Belgium	3 to 6 months
France	12 months
West Germany	6 to 12 months
Italy	6 to 12 months
UK	3 months minimum

By comparison the approval period achieved by the Federal Communications Commission in the USA is less than ten weeks and such approval provides access to the full US market.

In the spring of 1989, the Commission proposed a series of measures to liberalise and deregulate the Community's telecommunications sectors. These are highly controversial both because of the procedural route which the Commission proposes to use and because of the threat which some member states believe the proposals hold for national monopoly suppliers of telecommunications services. It is clear, however, that the benefits of harmonisation – particularly in association with deregulation – would be particularly great in this sector and would enable the development of a more competitive, but smaller, telecommunications equipment and switchgear industry in Europe.

10. Harmonisation of standards

Until 1985, the Commission pursued a detailed sector by sector approach to the replacement of national rules. This was not successful for three reasons:

- While 300 directives were adopted they were often out of date before they were completed as a result of market and technical changes

- The detailed process of item by item negotiation was very costly

- New national rules were being adopted much more rapidly than existing rules were being harmonised

In fact, the Community's first ambitious programme to eliminate technical barriers to trade was launched as far back as 1969. Typical of the programme were directives accompanied by detailed annexes setting out technical matters. As markets and technology advanced, these annexes had to be kept up to date and this proved to be a massive task. In time, the flow of new directives (each of which at that time had to be agreed unanimously by all the member states) dried up and it was 1985 before the Council of Ministers adopted a resolution setting out a **New approach** 'new approach' to technical harmonisation and standards.

There was, however, one important success in European harmonisation during the period. It was a directive drafted in a different way. The 1973 Low Voltage Directive was written in such a way that national standards, harmonised through CENELEC (Comité Européen de Normalisation Electrotechnique), would provide the detailed criteria for assessing the safety of a wide range of products against a list of minimal essential safety requirements in place of detailed annexes. This exceptional approach was to prove very influential when the Commission reviewed its work on technical harmonisation in the mid 1980s.

The Community role

By the mid 1980s, and with the renewed recognition of the importance of creating a single market, a new approach to technical harmonisation was clearly needed. This 'new approach' was agreed in 1984 and 1985. Under the 'new approach':

- Directives issued will take as a reference a high level of protection, thus ensuring that the new rules will not lead to a lowering of standards across the Community. The 'new approach' directive will set out the essential requirements for its implementation which are written in general terms and must be met before the product is liable for sale across the Community or in any national market. The European standards will then provide the required detail and be the key to European businesses fulfilling the essential requirements. The final element in the jigsaw will be the CE mark which will be the attestation that any product carrying the mark meets the essential requirements. Thereafter the product may be marketed anywhere in the Community. It will be a criminal offence to sell products which do not comply with the rules.

CE mark

- Harmonisation by the Community is to be concerned with the *objectives* not with the means.

- National authorities are to implement a common set of Community rules through their own regulatory systems.

- A qualified majority voting system was introduced in the Council of Ministers for adoption of directives.

There are three key phrases which have to be understood in any discussion of how this 'new approach' works. They are 'essential requirements', 'the principle of mutual recognition' and 'Article 36 of the Treaty of Rome'.

Essential requirements

Under the new approach the Commission has moved away from detailed product by product specification of specific technical requirements in directives towards specification (in broad terms) of the requirements which a product must have. These essential requirements specify what is necessary, for example, for the protection of public health and safety or for the protection of the environment. Such a 'new approach' directive does not, however, specify in detail how the essential requirements are to be implemented technically. That task falls to the European standards organisations CEN (Comité Européen de Normalisation) and CENELEC, which draw up the technical details in the form of European standards outside the Commission machinery on the basis of a consensus of those with an interest in the standard (national standards authorities, industry representatives, etc.).

Mutual recognition

The principle of mutual recognition means that a product lawfully produced and sold in one member state should be capable of being freely offered for sale in any other member state without having to be modified, tested, certified or renamed. This principle was established in the '*Cassis de Dijon*' ruling, which is perhaps the most famous decision in European law relating to technical barriers to trade. The case related to an attempt by West Germany to exclude French Cassis on the ground that its low alcoholic strength breached German regulations, but the Court found such regulations to be in breach of the Treaty of Rome and established the principle of *mutual recognition* which has since been the basis of most Community legislation in relation to barriers to trade.

Cassis de Dijon

Article 36 of the Treaty of Rome

The principle of mutual recognition breaks down both in law and in practice when it encounters the right of each member state to protect its essential interests in terms of issues such as public safety. That right is enshrined in Article 36 of the Treaty of Rome. This article means that if one country has a different approach to the protection of the environment or health and safety, then it may quite legitimately erect barriers to trade in the form of national regulations. In such circumstances the Community can break down the barriers only by the substitution of Community legislation for national legislation by means of making proposals to the Council which will be formalised after amendment into legislation. Until quite recently approval of a directive required unanimity among member states and the process was very slow. However, once a directive has been issued, no national legislation can prevent the sale of a good produced in accordance with its provisions.

As a result of all the above, the work of the Community on technical harmonisation now centres around the preparation of 'new approach' directives. These spell out the essential requirements to be met in those product areas in which the essential interests of member states (in terms of issues such as public safety and the protection of the environment) have in the past led to intractable differences in national requirements. In other areas, the priority is to achieve the mutual recognition of harmonised standards.

The making of a 'new approach' directive

Increasing pace

The Single European Act has affected the new approach in three ways:

- It amended the Treaty of Rome to allow directives to be adopted under Article 100A by a qualified majority of 54 out of 76 votes – the UK, France, West Germany and Italy each have 10 votes; Spain has 8; Belgium, Greece, the Netherlands and Portugal have 5; Denmark and Ireland 3; and Luxembourg 2.

- It introduced the 'co-operation procedure' which is intended to allow the European Parliament greater input to legislation before it is formalised. The Council cannot adopt a Common Position (a directive which has been considered and agreed by the Council but still awaits the opinion of the European Parliament and formal adoption by the Council) without taking into account the European Parliament's opinion of the Commission text. The European Parliament has another opportunity to express its view after a Common Position has been adopted, before the Council formally adopts it as Community law.

- It also amended the Treaty of Rome to allow directives relating to workplace health and safety to be adopted under Article 118A of the Treaty. Like Article 100A directives, those adopted under the provisions of Article 118A are adopted by the qualified majority voting system and are subject to the 'co-operation procedure'.

By 1 January 1990 six 'new approach' directives had been adopted under Article 100A. They relate to simple pressure vessels, electro-magnetic compatibility, toy safety, machinery safety, construction products and personal protective equipment. In addition, a common position has been reached on a directive relating to non-automatic weighing machines and draft directives are under discussion in relation to gas appliances, mobile machinery, lifting equipment and active implant medical devices. It is not expected that there will be many more directives under the new approach, but a series of four draft directives on medical equipment is planned for publication later in 1990, and a draft directive on lifting equipment amending the earlier Directive 89/392 is also planned. The Commission has also proposed six draft directives under article 118A. A common position has been reached on a draft framework directive and the other five drafts are under discussion. Two of them, relating to the use of machinery and of personal protective equipment, are intended to complement draft directives proposed under the provisions of Article 100A.

Progress in making 'new approach' directives was initially very slow, but is now speeding up. To summarise the position, 'new approach' directives have been accepted or are in the process of adoption in the areas listed below.

Product range	Essential requirements applying
	Agreed directives
Simple pressure vessels	Raw materials, welding materials, vessel design and accessories, manufacturing processes used and instructions supplied to users
Toy safety	Physical and mechanical properties, flammability, hygiene, radioactivity, chemical safety
Construction products	Mechanical resistance, stability, fire safety, hygiene, health and the environment, safety in use, noise standards, energy standards and heat retention
Personal protective equipment	Suitability of components, requirements relating to particular risks (e.g. fire, cold)
Machinery safety	Materials and products, lighting, fire, hazards relating to moving parts, noise, vibration, emissions, maintenance, indicator and instruction handbooks
Electro-magnetic compatibility	Avoidance of generation of electrical disturbances, immunity to the effects of such
	Directives under discussion
Measuring instruments	Units of measurement, accuracy, design and construction standards
Gas appliances	Materials, design, combustion and temperature
Implantable medical devices	Not yet determined
Active medical devices	Not yet determined
Lifting equipment	Not yet determined

The content of a 'new approach' directive

A 'new approach' directive is made up of the following seven elements:

Coverage

- A definition of the (generally very wide) range of products covered by the directive.

Essential requirements

- A statement of the essential requirements relating to safety etc., couched in general terms. Products must satisfy these essential requirements before they can be put on sale anywhere in the Community, *including the domestic market of the producer*. Since most 'new approach' directives are intended to cover a generic class of risks (electromagnetic compatibility, for example) more than one directive may apply to a particular product or class of products.

Methods of satisfying the essential requirements

- The normal method of satisfying the essential requirements will be by demonstrating compliance with a specified European standard. This, however, could act as a brake on innovation and new product design. There is, therefore, the opportunity for the manufacturer to demonstrate compliance with the essential requirements directly, perhaps by means of independent testing or certification. The use of standards will remain voluntary. Nevertheless, compliance with a standard is expected to be the normal means of demonstrating that a product conforms to the essential requirements of a directive.

Attestation

- Attestation of conformity to the essential requirements can be by declaration by the manufacturer, backed up by his own or independent test results; the certificate of an independent body;

test results of an independent body; or an acceptable variant of these methods. Products will carry the CE mark to demonstrate conformity.

The UK government has argued that a manufacturer's declaration – the least burdensome form of attestation – should be the preferred means of attestation unless it is shown that the risks involved in a particular case justify the expense of independent attestation.

Transitional arrangements

- Until a European standard has been made, or where no European standard is planned, national standards may be used as a means of demonstrating compliance, provided that the national standard has been approved by the Commission for that purpose.

Free circulation

- A product that has been properly attested as conforming to the essential requirements and has been CE-marked is entitled to free circulation throughout the Community.

Safeguard procedure

- A member state may prevent the placing of products on the market, or require their removal from the market, on the grounds that they do not in fact satisfy the essential requirements. If the product has been properly attested by the procedure above, it will have been presumed to be entitled to free circulation throughout the Community. In that case the member state must inform the Commission of its decision to withdraw the product, and the Commission will consult other member states and may find that the action taken was in breach of the Treaty of Rome.

The harmonisation process

The making of a directive is a long and complex process usually involving political and industrial bargaining over a period of years.

However, it is only the starting point of the process of removing technical barriers in a particular product range. A directive provides two key components of such action: a framework, in the form of specification of the essential requirements; and a fallback procedure in the form of the principle of free movement of goods which conform to the essential requirements or to national standards. The ending of technical barriers for a particular range of goods requires further action at both European and national levels to create European and national standards; to repeal, modify or update national regulations; and to establish mutually recognised testing, certification and inspection procedures.

Modifying national regulations to reflect the requirements of a directive is up to the national governments and legislatures of member states. It can be a lengthy and complex procedure and is subject to political influence in relation to how a directive is implemented. There is a danger that elements of protectionism will creep in this way, but the implementation by a member state of a directive is monitored by the Commission which may, ultimately, take action against an offending member state through the European Court of Justice. In the UK, the European Communities Act of 1972 sets out special procedures for legislation which implements the UK's obligations arising from membership of the Community.

Standards, testing and certification procedures

How a European standard is made

CEN and CENELEC

'New approach' directives rely heavily on the availability of European standards. The process of making standards is complex, even at national level. Because compliance with a standard is voluntary the process requires that a real effort is made to seek a consensus among interested parties on the content of the standard. This can take many years of work for a particular product or range of products. This process is even more complex at Community level where the range of producer interests is wider and different existing national standards have to be brought together. This process is managed by two organisations representing the major standard-setting authorities of Europe – CEN and CENELEC. Both organisations are based in Brussels but are independent of the Commission. Both bodies include the members of the European Free Trade Association (EFTA), in their membership and thus construct standards for a very significant part of world trade (357 million people). The existence of CEN and CENELEC reflects a historical separation in the making of international standards. There is, in addition, a separate International Organisation for Standardisation (ISO) and International Electrotechnical Commission (IEC).

The different national standards bodies in Europe, members of CEN and CENELEC, are represented on the ISO and the IEC. It is thus frequent to find European standards introduced alongside international standards. A list of the member bodies of CEN and CENELEC and of the national standards authorities can be obtained from the British Standards Institution (BSI) (see Appendix 9).

CEN and CENELEC operate under rules which are intended to align European standards with appropriate international standards, where they exist, and to achieve consistency between the national implementation of European standards. Procedures exist for qualified majority decision making by CEN and CENELEC (although these procedures do not automatically apply to EFTA members) and for simplified procedures to apply where a member state is applying a European standard in a way appropriate to national conditions.

In essence, CEN and CENELEC members provide secretariats through which European standard organisations can collaborate and reach decisions, but this system has a very heavy work-load, and individual product standards still require the involvement and contribution of producers from throughout the Community. As a result the process is very slow.

BSI
BSI is the UK member of CEN and CENELEC. The BSI, its library and its publications, provide a wide range of information on the application of the European standard-setting process to any particular situation. Setting standards in CEN and CENELEC is essentially a process of seeking consensus among the national members of the organisations. Once an acceptable text has been developed in a working technical committee, it is circulated to all the national member organisations for comment. The CEN or CENELEC committee reviews any resulting comments and the draft standard is circulated to members for adoption by a qualified majority voting system. All the national members have agreed to adopt the resulting European standard as their national standard (a British Standard in the UK) and to withdraw any conflicting national standards.

The main types of CEN and CENELEC publications are the *European Standards* (designated EN), *Harmonisation Documents* (designated HD) and *European Pre-standards* (ENV). ENs and HDs are CEN and CENELEC standards while the ENVs are prospective standards for provisional application and are akin to BSI's *Drafts for Development*.

ENs

An EN carries the obligation on CEN/CENELEC members to implement it at national level by giving it the status of a national standard and by withdrawing any conflicting national standards. The technical content of an EN is, therefore, presented in identical form in each country and is of equal validity (except, possibly, in EFTA countries whose members had not supported its adoption).

HDs

An HD carries the same obligation to withdraw any conflicting national standards but public announcement of its number and title is otherwise sufficient. HDs are established if transposition into national standards is unnecessary (as is the case when a CEN/CENELEC member has already adopted the ISO or IEC standard being endorsed in Europe) or impracticable, and particularly if agreement is subject to the acceptance of national deviations.

The BSI develops the UK position in these negotiations by seeking consensus in the corresponding BSI technical committee, which is made up of representatives of interested parties including producers, and BSI then argues this case in CEN and CENELEC. A list of the current BSI Standards Policy Committees is given in Appendix 7.

Those who participate most actively in the process of standard setting tend to have the greatest influence on the outcome. Individual firms can make recommendations to the BSI which will be taken into account by the BSI. If, however, a particular proposed standard has important implications for your firm, the best response is to make your views known through the appropriate trade association for your industry, which then carries their members' concerns directly to the BSI. BSI publishes the names of its staff responsible for particular issues. Your chamber of commerce or the CBI will also be interested in your views and will know how to advance them in consultation with the BSI. Contrary to popular opinion, the Commission is very open to effective and well informed lobbying. However, lobbying too late or too early, lobbying the inappropriate institution at a particular stage of the legislative process or indeed simply not approaching the largely overworked Commission staff in the right way can all be counter-productive. The DTI has produced a video called 'Brussels Can You Hear Me?' to assist British firms to carry out effective lobbying of the Commission. This is a task in which all firms, not only the very largest, can participate. More detail on the role of lobbying is given in Part III of this book.

Participation in CEN committees

By June 1990, CEN had 212 technical committees. The secretariat of fifty-nine of those committees was held by DIN (the West German standards organisation), AFNOR, (the French standards organisation) held the secretariat of a further forty-two and BSI held the secretariat of fifty. The views of British industry are argued in all cases but, in effect, the country providing the secretariat sets the agenda for a committee, so in some cases the views of West German and French industry may be given greater weight. Greater participation by industry is vital.

An example may help to illustrate the difficulties. The Community formally adopted the Construction Products Directive on 21 December 1988. As this is a 'new approach' directive, it merely sets the framework of essential requirements which products must meet. The detailed implementation of the Directive will fall to the standard-setting process. Member states have thirty months to give effect to the provisions of the Directive in both regulations and standards. Technical committees working under CEN are now starting work on preparing the draft standards, but there is, as yet, no agreement on the groups of products to which particular standards will apply and the pressure of work in relation to other directives is already slowing down the progress of CEN.

It is important to keep the process of setting European harmonised standards in the right perspective in relation to national standards setting. In 1987, work was initiated on 2,700 new standardisation projects in national standards organisations in Europe. In the same year, work was initiated on 660 new European standards. However, the European standards generally apply to a wider range of products than their national counterparts. Even at the present volume of European standard setting, the resources of CEN and CENELEC are under considerable pressure and the Commission has agreed to fund further staff for work on harmonisation of standards under Commission mandates.

ETSI and EWOS

In addition to CEN and CENELEC, there are two further standardisation bodies. They are the European Telecommunications Standards Institute (ETSI) and the European Workshop on Open Systems (EWOS), which is a working party attempting to define the Community's role in relation to work by the International Standards Organisation on the establishment of open systems interconnection standards in the information technology field. Both organisations are quite different in nature from CEN and CENELEC (i.e. they are product/industry based) and there is some debate as to whether they offer an alternative and better model for industry-based European standards harmonisation. They will almost certainly produce more rapid results, but the opportunities for replicating them in other sectors may be limited because they do not come from the same consensus-seeking and open tradition of standard making as CEN and CENELEC and their constituent national members.

In addition to the process of standard setting itself, there are three procedures or rules which it is useful to be aware of. They are:

- A procedure whereby work on developing *national standards* is subject to a 'standstill' when CEN or CENELEC put in hand the preparation of a harmonised European standard at the request of the Commission. This effectively prevents member states pre-empting the harmonisation procedure by varying national standards.

- Mutual information procedures. Under a directive (83/189 EEC) dating from 1983, member states are required to give the Commission written notification of the making of new technical regulations and standards. This procedure enables the Commission to step in to avoid the creation of new technical barriers to trade. This procedure has recently been extended to cover products such as foodstuffs, agricultural goods, medicines and cosmetics which were previously outside its reach. Even before its extension the level of notifications was of the order of 200 per annum.

- Use of European standards in public procurement. It is intended, with certain limited exceptions, that European standards will be applied in public procurement contracts and that contract specifications which make references to proprietary goods will be prohibited, unless such reference is the only way a product can be accurately described.

Mutual recognition of testing and certification procedures

Even when standards and regulations have been harmonised, it is necessary to ensure that technical barriers do not remain implicit in those additional testing and certification procedures which are frequently required by customers. Testing and certification procedures are in some industries the major form of technical barrier to trade but to date relatively little progress has been made in ensuring consistent and fair treatment. There are two principles underlying the work to date on harmonisation of testing and certification procedures. They are:

- In regulations; use of common standards of testing and certification including those for testing and certification organisations themselves.

- In other areas; mutual recognition of test results and certificates. It seems likely that mutual recognition of certifications will develop along sectoral lines as a result of practical co-operation but this may mean that not all member states will participate from the start of the arrangements. Mutual recognition of test results seems likely to develop as a separate arrangement.

It is likely that accreditation of a testing body under the proposed European standards will provide the basis for mutual recognition. In addition, the Commission with CEN, CENELEC and EFTA have set up a European Organisation for Testing and Certification and the Commission is preparing policy papers on testing and certification for discussion with the Council of Ministers, the Parliament and the Economic and Social Committee. All of this suggests recognition by the Commission that harmonisation of testing and certification arrangements is fundamental to the elimination of technical barriers to trade and, therefore, to the creation of the single market.

III
Marketing to Europe

11. Achieving the benefits – the reality

In contemplating marketing to the public sector and industry in Europe, it is easy to get carried away by statistics and surveys, all of which purport to indicate the existence of a massive market for your company's product or services. It is of fundamental importance to recognise that, for the vast majority of companies the correct strategic marketing advice regarding marketing into the public sector and industry in Europe is 'Proceed with caution'. The opportunities in the single market are considerable, but for many companies the existence of large, new markets may prove to be illusory.

Throughout Part III of this book we will be emphasising the importance of correct analysis and research before deciding on which new markets you wish to enter. In this chapter, we will particularly emphasise the reality behind achieving the benefits of scale discussed earlier in Parts I and II. Opportunities for increased economies of scale *will* result from the reduction of barriers to trade. However, many barriers to trade across Community borders will continue to exist – natural **Natural barriers** barriers, which no legislation can remove and which time may or may not erode.

In drawing up a marketing strategy for your company the first step is to recognise the difference between *artificial* and *natural* barriers to trade and the different effects they have on doing business in the Community. In this chapter, we will provide you with a simple grid model showing how artificial and natural barriers interact and their effect on various types of industry.

Artificial and natural barriers

Achieving the benefits of economic integration will be a major challenge given the scale and diversity of Europe and its long-standing and widely differing industrial practices. It is important to remember that, just as the European market is fragmented by the distortions introduced by the existence of twelve different member states, it is also fragmented by the natural differences in the nature of industries and the markets they serve.

These natural differences (or barriers) are fundamentally different from the artificial barriers to trade discussed earlier in this book. In particular, we have examined the artificial barriers to trade generated by widely differing public procurement practices and widely different technical standards. The impact of these two types of artificial barriers to trade is different from industry to industry. The degree of fragmentation in the market-place caused by artificial barriers is higher in more protected industries and those which are highly regulated (such as telecommunications and motor vehicle construction); the lower the degree of regulation, the less artificially fragmented is the market-place. A good example of an industry not particularly fragmented by **Personal services** artificial barriers is that of personal services (hairdressing, for example). In terms of artificial barriers to trade (procurement practices, technical standards, taxes, mobility of labour, etc.) there is little if anything to prevent a hairdresser from Milan travelling to London to ply his trade.

The thrust of the 1992 programme is, of course, to remove the fragmentation caused by artificial barriers in those highly protected and regulated industries mentioned earlier, and to give the Parisian telephone manufacturer or the Stuttgart car manufacturer similar access to sell his goods in other countries as that currently enjoyed by the Milanese hairdresser.

Much of the discussion of 1992 suggests that the removal of artificial barriers will signal the end of the fragmentation of European markets **European** and will lead to the creation of *integrated European markets* for all goods **integration** and services. It is further suggested that these single markets will be dominated by a few large producers serving wide Community markets with common products (and also competing more effectively at the international level). This *will* be true for a small number of very large businesses but, in practice, most businesses serve very local markets and will not wish (or will not be able) to extend their reach to a wider range of customers. In other cases different national tastes and/or circumstances (natural differences) mean that Europe will remain separated into reasonably distinct national markets.

Natural differences (or barriers) arise through national and local tastes, transport costs, geographical location and other factors against which there can be no legislation. It is essential to recognise that while legislation may be put in place which prevents the West German authorities from banning British beer on the grounds of ingredients or recipe, there is no accompanying legislation which insists that the German consumer must either like the beer, or buy it. Similarly, while our Milanese hairdresser faces very few, if any, artificial barriers to hairdressing throughout the EC, no legislation can either remove the high transport costs involved in travelling from one city to another or compel French consumers to appreciate Italian styling.

Market categories

While the impact of natural barriers is complex and unevenly spread, it is possible to categorise industries broadly into those which are highly fragmented through natural barriers and those which are not really impacted at all. Commodities (such as oil, for example) are not, by and large, affected by natural barriers to trade, unlike our previous example of personal services (such as hairdressing) which obviously are.

Understanding the impact of reducing the artificial fragmentation of markets (induced by differing technical standards and discriminatory public purchasing practices, for example) requires an understanding of the natural fragmentation of markets (induced by differing market conditions). In effect, as well as it being necessary to examine the artificial protection of particular national industries, it is equally necessary to understand the natural protection which particular markets may offer suppliers.

The most important issue is obviously whether your sector, firm or product is likely to be at risk or to benefit. An accurate analysis of this issue is critical to success in marketing to the European public sector or industry. To simplify such an analysis, it is possible to divide industries into three broad categories:

- Those which have an almost entirely *local or national market*, (e.g. personal and professional services)

- Those primarily serving *national markets* but *with a significant degree of trade* (e.g. clothing, consumer durables and food)

- Those serving *Community or international markets* (e.g. oil and other commodities, textiles, electronic goods and aerospace products)

Market reach The degree of *market reach* of an industry is a result of its customer base and the technology it employs. For example, in the retail sector the basic need is for a supplier to have outlets close to the customer. (Changes in technology are enabling mail order to make increased inroads into some parts of the retail sector, but for most products closeness to the customer is still the key issue.) The outlet may be owned by a national or international firm (Benetton or Marks & Spencer, for example) but must be *located* where the customer wishes to make his purchases.

The same is true for professional services. The major international accountancy firms have an international network, but they deliver their services through *local* offices providing *localised* services to *local* customers. In manufacturing, too, closeness to the customer may be important, in the 'white goods' sector, for example, but at the other end of the range there are industries where low costs of production are the dominant concern.

The impact of artificial and natural barriers

If we place these different degrees of *natural market fragmentation –* local or national, national with trade, and international – on the horizontal axis of a scatter diagram and make the vertical axis represent the degree of *artificial fragmentation* from which a sector suffers, the result is a grid on which can be marked the position of particular products or of industrial sectors (Figure 3).

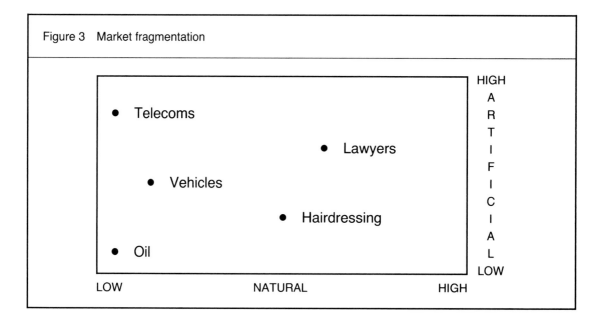

Figure 3   Market fragmentation

A number of points arise from this figure:

- It is possible to plot on the chart the position of your own firm or of particular products you produce. This is a useful start to analysing the implications of 1992 for your own firm.

- 1992 will have a two-fold effect on the position of a firm or product on the grid. General moves towards integration will move the position of a firm or product to the left (see Figure 4). The extent of this leftward move will depend on the sensitivity of the firm to changes such as investment in transport infrastructure within Europe or the increased ease of establishing subsidiaries in other member states.

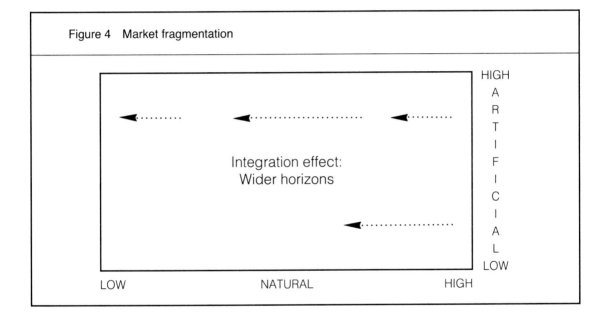

Figure 4   Market fragmentation

- A downward movement (see Figure 5) will occur because of the ending or reduction of technical barriers to trade and of discriminatory public purchasing practices. The degree and extent of both these movements (downward and leftward) will vary from industry to industry, from firm to firm, and from product to product.

  The combined effect will tend to be a movement from the top right-hand corner of the grid to the bottom left-hand corner (see Figure 6).

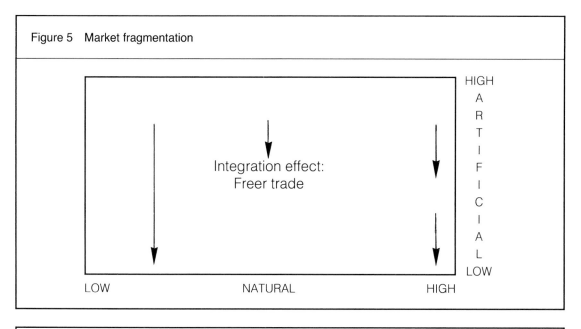

Figure 5 Market fragmentation

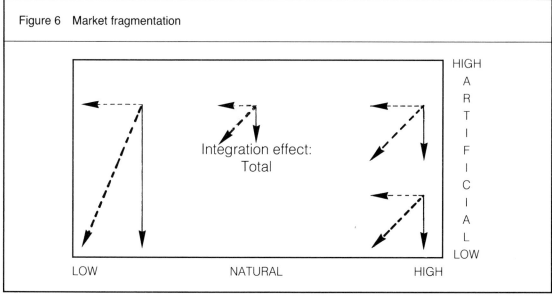

Figure 6 Market fragmentation

Sectors at risk and sectors likely to benefit

As stated above, the impact of artificial and natural barriers to trade will differ from industry to industry, from company to company and from product to product. In Figure 7 we have plotted where some industries may be on the grid and indicated some of the movement which industries will experience as a result of the 1992 programme. *Telecoms* and *vehicle manufacture* are industries which will benefit considerably from the reduction of the currently high artificial barriers to trade (mainly through differing technical standards). We have shown this as a downward movement on the grid. *Lawyers* are a group which will benefit from a reduction in the natural fragmentation of the market which is currently caused by the cultural non-acceptance of non-local legal advice. As industries become more and more pan-European, the use of lawyers from countries other than that of head office will not only be more acceptable, it may well be more positively encouraged. This results in a leftward movement on the grid. It could also be argued that the legal profession will also see a downward movement on the grid as EC-wide mutual acceptance of qualification criteria is imposed as part of the 1992 programme.

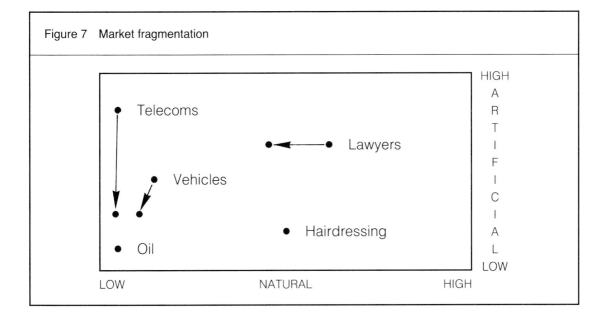

Figure 7   Market fragmentation

In order to analyse in more detail the likely effects of the 1992 programme in reducing artificial and/or natural barriers to trade, it is beneficial to split the grid into four quadrants. Firms located in *Quadrant A* will be *least affected* by 1992 because, although they operate in relatively open markets, they have a degree of natural protection on account of their proximity to their customers. Structural change in this quadrant is likely to occur mainly through mergers and acquisitions, not by growth of existing firms directly into new markets.

Figure 8   Market fragmentation

Quadrant C	Quadrant B
Protected 'national champions'	*Regulated 'local'*
Strengths: Little	Strengths: Local expertise/natural protection
Weaknesses: Overcapacity	Weaknesses: Lack of scale
Opportunities: Wider market	Opportunities: Broader horizons
Threats: New entrants	Threats: Competition
Effect of 1992 Massive	*Effect of 1992* Uncertain
Type of effect Rationalisation	*Type of effect* Reorganisation
• Restructuring, closures	
• Entry by non-EC firms	• Mergers, alliances, etc.
• Highly competitive	• Some new entry?
Quadrant D	**Quadrant A**
Open market industries	*Local services*
Strengths: Already competitive	Strengths: Natural protection
Weaknesses: Little	Weaknesses: Lack of scale
Opportunities: Growth of EC	Opportunities: Few
Threats: Increased attention	Threats: Few
Effect of 1992 Slight	*Effect of 1992* Very small
Type of effect Growth	*Type of effect* Ownership
• Continued competition	• Acquisitions
• Some entry by non-EC firms	• No additional new entry

HIGH — ARTIFICIAL — LOW (vertical axis)

LOW   NATURAL   HIGH

Firms located in *Quadrant B* will experience *significant changes* due to the reduction of the high artificial barriers to trade, but they will still enjoy a degree of natural protection because of the need to be close to customers. There will be increased opportunities for trading but again much of the change is likely to occur as a result of mergers and acquisitions.

Firms located in *Quadrant C* will face *major problems* in that they have enjoyed high artificial protection in markets with little natural protection and which would otherwise be open to international competition. It is in this quadrant that major structural adjustments are needed to reduce over-capacity. These firms are likely to experience severe price and cost competition but those which can sustain a competitive advantage (see Chapter 16) will have the ability to sell into newly open and vastly expanded European markets.

Firms located in *Quadrant D* are already *survivors*. They have already been competing in an open market exposed to the force of European and international competition. They will benefit from cost savings as a result of 1992 and from their increased ability to attack wider European markets. This is the quadrant where the classic economies of scale due to European integration are most likely to be realised.

Firms in both *Quadrant C* and *Quadrant D* will be exposed to considerably increased *competition from outside the EC*, as a result of the enlarged market. Third country firms (i.e. overseas, non-EC firms) will benefit as much as EC firms from the ending of artificial fragmentation of EC markets and are already increasing their investment in Europe because of their fear of a 'Fortress Europe' policy which exists in other major industrial nations. This phenomenon is explored in more detail in later chapters. Interestingly, where EC firms are for some reason not cost-competitive with those from other regions, then those third-party suppliers will reap most of the benefit of European integration.

Application to your company

This framework, while very much over-simplified, permits an analysis of the relative position of individual firms and individual product lines and it can lead to useful insights into alternative strategies for handling the changes which 1992 will bring.

Market position

As was outlined earlier, you should consider plotting not only your industry's position on the grid but also that of your company and, if appropriate, that of individual product lines. The analysis of the likely effect of the reduction of artificial and/or natural barriers as a result of the 1992 programme will be of particular benefit. You may well find that some products will benefit greatly from the reduction in artificial barriers to trade but may well still have considerable natural barriers to overcome. On the other hand, products with little or no natural barriers to trading throughout Europe may have a genuinely unified market opportunity as a result of the reduction of existing artificial barriers.

Application of any device like this grid is obviously subjective and you should present your analysis for review within your company, or to an independent outside adviser for a second opinion. Having arrived at a general understanding of the real impact of the reduction of artificial barriers to trade on your company, you can then begin to utilise the tools and strategies detailed in the rest of this book to devise your own market-led 1992 strategy.

One further point on the application of the grid. Artificial and natural barriers differ from member state to member state. Having applied the techniques outlined in Chapter 15, you should apply the grid analysis to each member state you have targeted as a market opportunity. You may well find that the extent of natural barriers in a specific market place is in itself a qualifying factor in deciding whether or not to enter that market.

12. Strategic marketing and the philosophy of change

In the previous chapter we saw that the market place will still be fragmented by natural barriers to trade long after artificial barriers have been reduced or eliminated entirely. In this chapter, we will be discussing the role of marketing within your organisation in meeting the challenge of the new European market after 1992. We will outline the underlying concept of strategic marketing, discussing where it fits within your organisation's overall activities, analysing the application of strategic marketing to the changes wrought by the single European market and, in particular, analysing how your marketing strategy can overcome (or at the very least, cope with) the fragmentation you will still meet throughout Europe. The chapter closes with specific guidance in formulating your marketing strategy to ensure it is specifically orientated to meeting the needs of European customers, and finally, a brief summary of the most common strategic marketing errors encountered by organisations attempting to enter new markets.

Strategic marketing

The basic function of marketing activities is to bring together buyers and sellers. At the most fundamental level, marketing activities, if treated in isolation, may ensure a repetition of this basic transaction – buyer meeting seller – for a relatively long period of time. However, most trading organisations are complex, and the market in which they trade even more so. *Strategic marketing* ensures that an organisation's marketing activities do not act in isolation, but as an integral part of the organisation's overall activities.

The basic concept of 'strategy' was originally developed in the context of war. Businessmen, like generals and politicians, must develop appropriate strategies to meet their overall objectives. Since it was appropriated for use in the business environment, 'strategy' has been defined and redefined many times. In the context being used here, *strategic marketing* consists of three basic steps:

1. The development of fundamental long-term goals and objectives

2. The assessment, choice and implementation of specific courses of action, geared to the attainment of those goals

3. The allocation of the required resources necessary to complete the chosen course of action

The importance of strategic marketing (as opposed to what might be termed simple marketing) is heightened when companies operate in a changing, fluid market place. Selling into a static market place is a relatively simple exercise – having established a competitive edge and strong customer relationships, the only remaining issue is to ensure that it is difficult for competitors to enter your market place. However, in the context of 1992 and the single market, we have seen that the market place is likely to continue to be diverse, rapidly changing, and subject to a wide range of pressures – legislative, political and economic. In this environment, the organisation which does not have a strategic marketing plan and which does not clearly lay out its overall objectives, and does not remain single-minded in the attainment of those objectives, will find itself confused, disorientated and easily left behind by customer and competitor alike.

Strategic marketing and the single market

If the advent of the single market and/or the changes in public procurement policies lead your company to consider strategic marketing for the first time, you should examine the implications in detail. The following guidelines will give you some idea of what will be involved.

It will be necessary for you to assess your strategic marketing requirements first of all in the light of your existing activities in your domestic market place. Having done that, you can return to these guidelines to develop the changes that will be required in your strategic marketing plan to incorporate the marketing activities you will undertake in your proposed new European markets.

For most companies, then, the post-1992 European environment will not dictate fundamental changes in overall strategies. Horizons may be widened and markets may become larger, but the basic objectives will probably remain the same. Strategic changes are more likely in organisations where access to a wider European market place brings a material, incremental change to the organisation itself – for example, where a company decides to move from full manufacture of all its products to sub-assembly or the use of licensed agents in other countries, in order to cope with the increased volumes required. The approach to some of these fundamental changes is discussed in Chapters 15 to 18. In broad terms, any company which anticipates undergoing such radical re-thinking at a strategic level should ensure that it has sought appropriate internal and external consulting expertise to audit its intentions and decisions.

We have already seen that the main purpose of developing a marketing strategy (as opposed to simply marketing) is to enable the organisation to cope with the process of change. Not only will the changes outlined in this book impact on marketing strategy, but fiscal, technological and manpower issues will all be involved. Consequently, it is the company which has the most flexible marketing strategy which will survive.

There are two particular processes of change which will need to be addressed by your company if it is to market itself successfully to the public sector and industry throughout the EC:

1. The process of *consolidation* of industries through mergers, acquisitions and the formation of strategic alliances

2. The *fragmentation* of the market place

Consolidation

One of the major underlying thrusts of the 1992 programme and the creation of a single market is the desire to enable industry to realise many of the economies of scale lost as a result of the fragmentation of national markets. In anticipation of this, and in order to retain worldwide competitive positions, there has been a general trend towards consolidation within many industries. This consolidation has taken two forms:

- The centralisation of manufacturing and/or distribution activities within individual companies, to produce a fewer number of larger units. This is often accompanied by incremental cost savings in labour or equipment costs, or both. Ford of Europe and Philips NV are good examples of major organisations which have anticipated this trend within the EC.

- Industries themselves are consolidating through mergers and acquisitions, and strategic alliances of various forms. Banking, accountancy and confectionery are all industries which have seen radical restructuring in this regard in recent years.

Any such fundamental restructuring, whether of an individual company or the industry within which that company competes, has a fundamental impact on the company's entire strategy, not least in marketing programmes and organisations. In reviewing the impact of the single market on your company's strategic marketing plan, the issue of consolidation needs to be considered in three ways:

- *Consolidation within your company* – Consolidation of manufacturing and/or distribution activities is more likely to be a financial decision than marketing-driven, and will be considered as part of the overall business plan drawn up in anticipation of single market entry. On the other hand, consolidation by way of merger, acquisition or strategic alliance is generally a market-driven issue. In the twelve member states, there were 117 mergers and acquisitions in 1983. According to the EC Directorate General on Competition, this increased to around 450 in 1988. The reasons for this level of activity are by nature complex, but are generally associated with market entry or maintaining market dominance. These issues will be discussed in more detail in Chapters 15 and 16. For a comprehensive examination of the whole topic of mergers and acquisitions, see *Mergers, Acquisitions and Alternative Corporate Strategies* (Hill Samuel Bank Limited) in this series.

- *Consolidation within your industry* – If there is a general wave of consolidation within your industry, then you must consider the position of your competitors. What steps are they taking to address the issues outlined above? Do you need to mirror their activities or react to them? Most importantly, what impact on your marketing programme does, say, the merger of two of your major competitors have? The grid diagram on p. 84 indicates some of the industries in which this form of restructuring is taking place. If your company is within the appropriate grid quadrant, then your strategic marketing plan will have to take account of these competitor changes.

- *Consolidation amongst buyers* – Every industry which goes through a process of consolidation is some other industry's customer. The move towards fewer, larger confectionery manufacturers means a reduction in the number of customers available to commodities growers. This consolidation of customers has an obvious two-way effect on a strategic marketing plan. First of all, the number of decision makers to be accessed within the single market should generally reduce and the 'key account' concept may well enjoy a revival amongst sales managers. This aspect is discussed further in Chapter 18. On the other hand, companies must continue to be aware of the impact of customer mergers and alliances in their own domestic market. If your 'own' customers at home are being taken over by, or are merging with other European companies, you may well find that the long-standing relationship that you had is quickly dissolved, or at least attacked by your European competitors who currently supply the acquiring or merging European firm.

The process of consolidation is one of the strongest undercurrents in European business today. To fully understand its impact on your company or organisation may require detailed analysis on a market by market basis. It would, however, be foolish to ignore it. Any medium-sized accountancy firm, for example, trying to break into the wider European market, will find that consolidation in the industry has *already* resulted in the barriers to market entry being considerable.

Fragmentation

It may seem strange, after detailing the many ways in which the 1992 programme seeks to remove barriers to trade within Europe, to raise the issue of fragmented markets. There are, however, a number of very good reasons why companies may find themselves selling into a fragmented market:

- *Lack of experience in exporting* – For many organisations, marketing into Europe will be their first step outside their domestic market place. Consequently, differences in culture, taste, language and natural barriers to trade will give rise to a fragmented market place.

- *High transportation costs* – Companies operating in industries with high transportation costs – cement, liquids, chemicals and most service industries – are limited in the size of the market they can serve from any other plant production location.

- *High stockholding costs* – In the same way as high transportation costs limit a company's ability to service the available market, so high stockholding costs prevent the construction of very large production facilities to service the whole market.

- *Unique buying requirements* – Local requirements, or needs, may well result in a high degree of product differentiation from member state to member state. Regional differences may well fragment the market even further. Ambulances, for example, are constructed to almost unique designs from country to country and often have further customisation requirements required by each local health authority. As a result, each ambulance sold is more or less unique.

Overcoming fragmentation

The four examples above give some indication of the wide range of causes of market fragmentation within the single market. Overcoming fragmentation will be one of the most significant strategic marketing opportunities available to any organisation wishing to sell into Europe. The benefits achieved in consolidating an otherwise fragmented market place can be very high if achieved. As we have seen, the single market programme will not in itself achieve this consolidation – your organisation or company will need to build market consolidation tactics into its strategic marketing plan. To do this successfully will require a detailed analysis of the likely areas of market fragmentation you will meet, coupled with an action plan of steps to be taken to overcome, or cope with, fragmentation. Some of the actions that might be undertaken to neutralise market fragmentation include:

- *Standardisation of market needs* – The ambulance manufacturer may reap considerable benefits from long-term lobbying and customer liaison to produce a more standardised vehicle requirement. In the short to middle term, producing a new product to supersede the old may help to coalesce individual buyer requirements. The modularisation of product manufacture, together with a reduction in available customised options, might achieve similar results.

- *Non-owned market delivery* – Many aspects of market fragmentation can be neutralised by creatively addressing the delivery of the product or service to the market place. Fast food restaurants, for example, were historically limited in scale by the requirement to be close to the customer, and to therefore have large numbers of outlets, all requiring expensive capital funding. This was overcome by franchising of units to independent owner-operators in the locality, with the original restaurateur earning a return by way of royalties. Estate agencies and financial services have developed along similar lines. High transportation and stockholding costs can be overcome by the use of manufacturing under licence and agency relationships in the target markets.

- *Acquisitions and mergers* – The role of acquisitions and mergers in consolidation has already been discussed, suffice it to say that one of the quickest ways to obtain expertise, critical mass and local knowledge in one transaction, is to identify an appropriate acquisition or merger.

Formulating your strategy to meet the needs of European customers

Developing a strategic marketing plan is a complex activity. In order for it to effectively interact with the other activities within the organisation, it must take into account production, finance, management, labour and a host of other complicating factors, some of which have been discussed above. In all of this process, it is remarkably easy to lose sight of the person for whom all of this activity is being undertaken – the customer.

Planning your product

Consideration of the changes in your strategic marketing plan must take account of the impact on your customers. It is imperative to remember that the 1992 programme *concentrates on supply rather than demand*. Community legislation will make markets available – it will not make them similar. This means that your strategic marketing plan will have to take account of often widely differing customer preferences and buying patterns across national boundaries. It is now a well-known example that French customers prefer top-loading washing machines, while their British counterparts tend to use front loaders, while the Germans differ from the Italians in preferring higher priced, high powered machines.

So, while in the long term, a general shift towards more standardised consumer preferences may occur, for the time being your company's strategic marketing plan must address the specific needs of your European customers, if it is to be successful. Your planning process, therefore, must include the following:

- *Market-specific research* – A hypothetical marketing strategy, written from a desk in Head Office, will not begin to assess the needs of the European customer accurately. Specific market and field research must be undertaken (Chapter 14).

- *Local involvement* – Any tourist knows the added value that can be obtained from a holiday by the use of a knowledgeable guide. Learning any new sport, be it golf, cricket, or soccer, is almost impossible without the assistance of someone who knows and regularly plays the game. Similarly, market entry, particularly across national boundaries, is almost impossible without the assistance of local knowledge to obtain the highest level of on-the-ground information. The use of local chambers of commerce, educational establishments, government departments and companies in your own supply chain all helps towards the process of developing a truly relevant marketing strategy. It is important not to restrict the use of local knowledge to basic research and checking of facts; identify individuals or organisations in your target market place with whom you can have a relationship of trust and have them audit your conclusions and perhaps even your overall objectives.

- *Follow industry trends* – While industries do tend to develop similarly from country to country, it is often the case that some countries are chronologically ahead or behind others in development. The statistical chance that your domestic industry is the most advanced in the industry is highly unlikely. It is therefore imperative that your strategic marketing plan anticipates industry trends in each of your target markets. Again, the use of local knowledge and specific market research is important. This should be coupled with participation in industry bodies if open to you, and the provision of accurate and concise summaries of trade articles, competitor product information and research documents where available.

- *Product testing* – To be successful, no strategic marketing plan can be constructed in a vacuum. Conclusions and prioritised actions must be a result of real interaction *with* the market place, not just an analysis of it. No assessment of the needs of your proposed European customers should be complete without appropriate product or service testing, where possible.

Strategic marketing that isn't

There are a number of specific (and common) strategic errors that should be avoided if your strategic marketing plan is to last beyond the short term:

- *Trying to be number one* – Market dominance has a beguiling attraction. If you are already dominant in your particular industry, across all the markets you intend to sell into, then a protection of that market dominance should be the central focus of your marketing strategy. If, however, you are dominant in your domestic market and intend to sell into new European markets, then an objective to obtain overall market dominance in any or all of those new markets should be considered very seriously before inclusion in your marketing strategy. All of the causes of market fragmentation discussed above will mitigate against an early or easy transition from domestic to European dominance and, while the pride of the marketing director may well be at stake, an achievable and sustainable long-term marketing strategy is much more important.

- *Doing it all from head office* – The importance of personal service and local knowledge, coupled with close control of the distribution operations and an awareness of trends and buyer requirements on the ground, have all been emphasised before. A wholly centralised marketing structure may well seem attractive from the perspective of control and interaction with other functions, but it will drive away accurate and relevant knowledge of the market. Although often adopted for cost reasons, a centralised marketing structure, if proposed, will almost always be seen to be a false economy in the long run.

- *Underestimating local competition* – A common error in the competitive analysis included in marketing strategies is the tendency to concentrate on competitors of a similar or larger size, and to underestimate the many small, private, or owner-managed firms which exist in other national markets. The assumption is often that the arrival of a new entrant in the market place will reduce margins and drive out many of these smaller firms. However, in practice, their overhead structure is often such that they can remain flexible and light on their feet, adjusting to reduce profits for a considerably longer period than anticipated. In addition, these companies often have strong supplier and buyer relationships which can be exceptionally hard to dislodge.

- *Honeymoons that last for ever* – Most companies want any new marketing initiatives to be successful. There is therefore an endemic tendency to interpret almost all test results on market research in a favourable light. This is recognised by most organisations and there is usually some form of audit or peer review to ensure that a strategy is not built on overly ambitious or optimistic basic assumptions. Nevertheless, it is a remarkably common fault that most companies fail to discount the 'honeymoon' effect of a new product or service's entry to the market. Products introduced to what may be already a very competitive market place are often initially received with great enthusiasm, resulting in a rapidly growing demand curve and strong early buyer interest. Indeed, such may be the enthusiasm for more information, or even better, more product, that the company increases its overhead to respond adequately. Typically, in such an environment (particularly where strong competition previously existed), other suppliers will catch up with demand and/or product innovation, and the new entry's demand curve shifts radically downwards.

While companies often anticipate such a honeymoon period for new products, it is often overlooked when an existing product – already established in its domestic market – is introduced into a new market place. The assumption is that the company is on to a winner. This is one reason why product testing should be concluded at a stage immediately before the conclusion of the strategic marketing process and its results included in the development of the strategic plan.

13. Creating a market-led organisation

The prospect of a single market post 1992 will cause many organisations to rethink their marketing strategy. Some of the more fundamental ways in which marketing strategies could be made more effective were discussed in the previous chapter. Coupled with these fundamental strategic changes must be a commitment to ensuring that the products delivered to the single market meet the European customer's needs. Some of the more mechanistic issues involved were also discussed in the previous chapter. However, the single most important method to ensure that any organisation meets the needs of its customers is to ensure that the *organisation*, not just the strategy, is market-led.

In this chapter, we will look at what it means to be a market-led organisation, explore some of the cultural issues which this will imply for your organisation, and look specifically at two areas which must be addressed to ensure that your company is market-led: organisation structure and marketing information systems.

Being market-led

There has been much emphasis laid throughout the 1980s on the importance of organisations being market-led. In terms of clearly defining what this means, it is much easier to state what it is *not*. A company or organisation is not market-led if it is product-led, engineering-led or finance-led. British Rail is an example of an organisation which has struggled to move from being engineering-led to market-led. Communications companies have in some cases moved full circle during the 1980s from being market-led to finance-led and back again.

Production-led companies stress the importance of the product and tend to employ most resources in product development and innovation, often at the expense of understanding market needs. Product-led management will often insist that they know best what the customer wants – Henry Ford's philosophy on the model T ('You can have it any colour you want as long as it's black') is a classic example of this.

Sales-led organisations emphasise sales maximisation at the expense of tracking consumer preferences. Pushing the company's product on the customer tends only to work for a limited period of time and consequently high promotional spending, hyper-active sales teams and bust or boom sales cycles dominate these types of company.

Finance-led organisations will often emphasise the immediate bottom line at the expense of product development and research. 'If the customer is buying it now, then keep making more' is often the philosophy, preventing long-term investment in a stream of new products or services matched to the customer's needs.

The successful company

The successful marketing-led company will counterbalance these differing pressures to ensure that it not only meets the needs of the customer, but is both profitable in the short term and investing for profits in the long term. The marketing-led company will typically focus on added value as opposed to simple bottom-line profits, because it is out of added value that investment decisions will be made regarding research and development, and real increases in added value will ensure long-term success. In particular, a profit-oriented, marketing-led company will shun sales volume for its own sake. Companies faced with the attraction of the newly accessible single market, may well find the magnetic pull of volume sales to be a false illusion, drawing them on to the rocks of over-trading and spiralling costs, downgraded quality and a ruined customer reputation.

It is in this environment that the company committed to marketing to the public sector and industry throughout Europe will ensure that it not only addresses the strategic marketing issues detailed in the previous chapter but also implements the organisational and information changes necessary to turn it into a truly market-led organisation.

Organisational culture

A firm commitment to building or maintaining a market-led company will involve not only changing structures and information flows, but also seeing through changes in the very nature of the organisation itself. Particularly for companies which have historically traded only in a domestic market and which are anticipating breaking into new markets for the first time, the biggest challenge will be a simple one – doing things differently. Although marketing into Europe does not change any of the fundamentals of good business in any of the main disciplines (marketing, finance, production and so on), it does mean that much of the company's culture will come under pressure. For a company moving from domestic market sales only into sales in other member states, three particular pressures on corporate culture should be expected – loss of centralised power, a need for collaboration and the use of cross-functional teams.

Loss of centralised power

Resistance may well be felt from head-office functions which have developed domestically over many years. The drive to relocate marketing and other functions in target markets (see below) will produce uncertainty and insecurity if it is not handled properly. The commitment of top management to explanation and education must be as strong as the commitment to implementation. Care should be taken to ensure that any transfer of power from central to regional locations is accompanied by the installation of strong information flows to ensure continued close co-operation with the functions transferred. This aspect is covered in the later section on marketing information systems.

The need for collaboration

The importance of local knowledge and local involvement in developing market strategies, market entry and the gathering of basic market information has been emphasised in earlier chapters and will be returned to again and again as a recurring theme. For a company accustomed to trading in one market, perhaps for a prolonged period, where senior managers have over the years accumulated detailed market knowledge for themselves, the concept of using outside assistance can often be hard to accept. In many companies (and sometimes in whole industries) there is a feeling that internal managers know their market better than anyone else, and this is often accompanied by a disdain for anyone who has not worked in the industry for a long period. It is essential that marketing directors and managers regularly emphasise the need for collaboration with agents, consultants, suppliers (and occasionally competitors), who are active in the target markets.

While a head-office team despatched, say, from Bristol to Liverpool may succeed in producing a relevant self-contained market analysis of that area (although even this is unlikely), sending the same team to, say, Bonn, will, on its own, achieve little.

The use of cross-functional teams

Collaboration will be required *internally* as well as externally. The mature organisation trading over a prolonged period in a domestic market will often find that its individual, functional disciplines (marketing, finance, production, etc.) have developed distinct and almost isolated identities, working in common only as far as is necessary to maintain a current market share. Selling across boundaries in the single market will require the use of cross-functional teams to integrate the marketing function with the rest of the company's activities. As will be seen later, the very method of trading in each member state may vary (manufacturing, manufacturing under licence, franchise, agency relationship). Cross-functional teams will be vital to analyse the impact of these and other issues, and to ensure that the company's marketing activity is suited to each market-place.

Organisation structure

The 1992 programme is creating a climate of change. Companies are reviewing extensive changes in their marketing programmes and strategies, and it is obvious, therefore, that organisations should also re-examine how appropriate their marketing *organisations* are to implement their revised marketing strategies.

Specific requirements

While every organisation will have its own specific requirements, and will need to review its organisation structure (perhaps with outside assistance) in the light of the changes brought about by the 1992 programme, there are some general trends which should be noted. While your company may be an exception to any or all of the following, your organisational structure review should take account of:

- *The need to standardise* – The continuing fragmented nature of the single market, even after the implementation of the 1992 programme, has been emphasised frequently in previous chapters. None the less, in order to extract maximum advantage from economies of scale, an effective marketing strategy should put its emphasis on the search for similarities or standardisation of preferences across national boundaries. As we have seen earlier, the reduction of adaptation costs and a modularisation of production will be important in maximising added value.

  Managing this process effectively has important implications for the marketing organisation structure of a company trading across national boundaries. In essence, it underlines the need to ensure that top management is undertaken on a pan-European basis, and not on a country-by-country basis. While regional managers will have increasingly important roles to play, ultimate management of a market strategy must be undertaken on a pan-European basis. Marketing directors will need to combine a breadth of vision – looking for ways to consolidate the market to achieve economies of scale through standardisation – with a sympathetic understanding of consumer preferences in national markets.

- *Regionalisation of functions* – Historically, regional offices performed sales (and perhaps administrative) functions only. It is now becoming more common for regional offices to have expanded responsibilities including marketing. The regional offices interact with the centralised, pan-European marketing function by submitting local input and developing marketing programmes specific for their area.

- *Emphasis on regional rather than country units* – As the geographic impact of national boundaries becomes less relevant, companies are tending to consolidate disparate country offices into fewer, larger regional offices. Honeywell is an example of a company which has dissolved many of its former country units in this way. Regional offices may take in two or more countries and occasionally include parts of countries which are economically similar. Alternatively the choice of regions may mirror the coverage and spread of locations of key customers.

- *Relocation of head offices* – In extreme cases, it may be appropriate to move the whole of the head office function to be closer to the customer, sources of decision making or new manufacturing facilities. As a company's marketing profile in Europe matures, one of the regional offices may become a *de facto* head office as a result of its gravitational mass. Flexibility in the company's organisation structure should allow for a realistic, market-based review of this issue at regular intervals – say, every three to five years.

- *The development of the European manager* – As a company's profile within European markets matures, and successful collaboration on a local basis produces an effective marketing strategy, it is likely that recruitment and training will emphasise less and less the importance of indigenous staffing of the marketing function. The search for product standardisation, coupled with the gradual harmonisation of professional qualifications and the need to have more self-contained regional offices will probably lead to the emergence of management development and training programmes geared towards creating marketing executives who are more broadly based, geographically experienced, and more mobile than previously.

Many of these tends will only be seen over the medium to long term. For many companies, perhaps intending to sell only into one or two non-domestic European markets, they will hardly be noticed at all. They should however be tracked, and the company's organisation structure should be flexible enough to accommodate the pressures induced by such trends.

Special pressures

There are two categories of business which are facing entirely separate organisation structural pressures as a result of the 1992 programme:

- *Third country businesses* – Companies and industries from third countries (i.e. outside Europe, notably the USA and Japan), wary of the development of a 'Fortress Europe' have gone against the overall trend of industry consolidation by rushing to locate in all of the significant European markets before the completion of the 1992 programme. Particular examples are Japanese banking and Near Eastern/Far Eastern assembly plants.

  Instead of reaping the organisational benefits of consolidation, through regionalisation, many such companies are now over-represented and over-staffed, and some degree of shake-out can be expected as the 1992 programme attains completion.

- *European multinationals* – European companies which are already trading on a multinational scale are in general consolidating faster than the industry average, collapsing subsidiary country offices into regional offices, often leaving sales and service facilities only on a country by country basis. Multinational companies which have multinational customers are in a much stronger position to take a genuinely pan-European approach to marketing, particularly in industries which have more or less standardised requirements. For these companies, with the resources to implement IT strategies to ensure effective centralised communications, sales forces are increasingly being organised on a product-line basis with senior sales personnel taking on smaller product portfolios across wider regional boundaries. The computer industry is a good example of this: when Brown Boveri of Switzerland merged with ASEA of Sweden, DEC won the majority of the newly merged company's computer business by combining its two account teams to reflect the 'new' customer's requirements.

Marketing information systems

It should have already become clear to any organisation intending to market to the public sector and industry in Europe that there will be a quantum leap of information to be managed. The marketing function's increase in information flow will be exacerbated by the widely different nature and indeed language of the information to be managed (see Chapter 14).

To maintain or create a market-led organisation, it is vital that there is a dependable *marketing information system*. Just as marketing on its own is of less relevance if it is not placed within the context of an overall marketing strategy, so the existence of information in a raw state is of much less benefit than information which has been systematically processed.

Work patterns

Business managers typically move from one problem to another, dealing with crises – major or minor – and finding little time to address broader issues. Marketing managers are no less guilty of dealing with the urgent rather than the important – being reactive rather than proactive. This is not surprising, as the marketing function works within the company's most fluid environment, providing many variable factors which can generate such major or minor crises. A lack of systematic processing of the information available to marketing decision makers is a root cause of the inability to become proactive, and can lead to market stagnation or (worse still) wrong decisions resulting in loss of market share.

MIS

To prevent this, a market-led organisation will implement a marketing information system (MIS). There is simply a recognised set of procedures which will ensure that information from whatever source (market research, market intelligence, internal records) are gathered, analysed and evaluated on a systemised basis, producing relevant, accurate and timely information for use by marketing decision makers. In a small- or medium-sized company, the MIS may take the form of regular sales reports and marketing information submitted by a small number of managers, which are reviewed by a director with marketing responsibility and presented as a written combined sales and marketing report on a monthly basis. A large company may have a sophisticated computer system which regularly collates marketing research produced internally and externally, summaries of external marketing intelligence (gleaned from trade journals and other authoritative sources), combines these with historic sales and, using a database of customer information, produces regular updated, sophisticated models of forecasted sales and marketing out-turns. In any case, your company should – with outside help if necessary – ensure that some system relative to your size and needs, exists to process marketing information. In the next chapter we will discuss some of the problems which will be met in attempting accurately to process information which is received from a variety of sources.

14. Getting the information right

It is the natural barriers that will continue to exist after the technical barriers come down which many companies trading in the EC will have to overcome. Each member state (and in many cases each region within a member state) will have certain preferences, not only in design of products but also in the way in which they are sold and distributed. These are all areas in which information will be essential if a smooth sales and marketing operation is to be launched.

Market research and the gathering of market information are only two of the key factors in successful marketing in the EC. They are, however, the basis for the whole strategic process detailed in Chapter 5 and it is vital that they are done well. This will take time, resources and investment, not just here in the UK, but also in the markets into which you wish to sell.

Much of the information required will be available only from local market sources. The gathering of specific local information in Europe will not be easy. In many cases the information source will be difficult to find; the precise information may not be available; information and data will probably be in a format with which you are not familiar and may not be compatible with information already gathered from other member states; in most cases it will be in the language of the member state in question. All these problems are going to be new and challenging to any companies engaging in non-domestic marketing for the first time.

In this chapter, we will review some of the basics of information gathering for the marketing of your products or services to the public sector and industry in Europe, and discuss some of the sources which you might use. A few guidelines will follow on how to avoid some of the problem areas that will be met in gathering information in Europe and finally, specific pointers will be given with regard to collating information in the field of public procurement. This chapter does not provide a detailed listing of all information sources – it aims to point you in the right direction for the collation of information. Further useful addresses are given in Appendix 9.

Basics

The basics of successful market research in Europe are no different to the basics in the domestic market. The two major functions are assessing new markets for products, and assessing new products for markets. To evaluate these two questions a company needs to look at:

- An assessment of the market's potential

- The limits of market accessibility (artificial/natural barriers)

- The most suitable mode of entry (export, licensing, joint marketing arrangement, joint venture, etc.)

- An analysis of existing competitors and those likely to come into the market after 1992

- An evaluation of the competitor's products – packaging and price

- An outline of the local marketing infrastructure and methods

Different companies and different industrial sectors will obviously require different types of information (financial, demographic, economic, market). Once the nature of the information required is established, the specific research may well be best carried out by (or at least augmented by) local nationals in the member states concerned. It may be worth engaging a professional market research organisation to do some of the work on your behalf and to assist you in the breakdown and the interpretation of your results. The assumptions underlying the interpretation of the information need to be noted in order to identify the rationale around which the conclusions were drawn. It is particularly important to subject any fundamental market assumptions to an independent or peer review.

While collecting information and undertaking basic market research, it is vital constantly to bear in mind the nature of the output required. If you have a sophisticated marketing information system (see previous chapter) the format output (at least) will be defined. If the MIS is more basic, output may well vary according to the organisation's current needs. One way to ensure confusion is to attempt to shoe-horn raw information into a unified format, when the information has been gathered for a different purpose. For example, subjective opinion on competitors' strategies may well be a vital element in the drawing up of market entry strategy, but it should not be presented as hard statistical data and may not sit well with a regular monthly analysis of, say, historical market share.

Sources

We have already seen that as 1992 approaches the amount of information available and the sources of information are going to increase. Already the diversity of information sources is a major hindrance to obtaining good quality information quickly. As we have seen, companies will require some type of MIS. Whether this is a computerised system or a member of staff is of no consequence as long as it is effective and relevant to your size and needs.

Part of that MIS should be a database of sources of information. This should contain not only the names and addresses from which information can be sought, but a brief indication of the nature of the information, its frequency and the use to which it should be put, together with any accompanying notes necessary for effective interpretation of the information. This database can be anything from a loose-leaf notebook to a sophisticated computer program, but it should be initiated right at the start of the information-gathering process, otherwise the sheer volume of information will strangle the decision-making process.

Detailed below are some of the EC-specific information sources you may wish to consult. The addresses of the institutions and organisations mentioned in this chapter are listed in Appendix 9 along with other useful sources of information. They should be treated as starting points only for your own enquiries.

DTI offices

If you are a newcomer to marketing in Europe, the best place to start is your local DTI office. Most offices have business libraries and database facilities. You can search the DTI's own database (BOTIS) for information on products and markets, overseas agents, distributors and importers, export opportunities, promotional events and for an index to other published information.

Export intelligence service

EIS is a computerised system designed primarily to give companies an advance warning of trade opportunities in your markets and for your products. It is a subscription service, and details of how to subscribe are available from your regional DTI office. (There are numerous services of this type available, which are either subscription or buy-as-you-use services.)

Tenders Electronic Daily

TED is an industry-specific database which updates client companies on the member states' government tenders available in their specific industry sectors, as they appear in the OJ (S section). The use of computer databases to scan and lift information is a growing phenomenon within the Community. It is interesting to note that the nature of the method of presentation of information on screen, and the accessing of information by use of key words and phrases, does tend towards information gathering in very precise areas. For these reasons, and because the cost of using computer databases is often related to time spent using the system, it is less likely that users will stray outside their generally defined areas for information requested. So, if you are going to use a database like TED, ensure that you also read the OJ (S section). This way you will see if there are any opportunities outside of those you might select on the database, which may not be industry/product specific but which may represent a parallel market opportunity. More information on the use of TED is provided in the later section on information on public procurement.

The OJ

The *Official Journal of the European Communities* is a must for all companies involved in public procurement. The OJ outlines all tenders available from member states in basic detail. It also lists who has received the tenders after they have been allocated (see p. 114).

The sales/supply chain

Information from sales and supply chains can prove invaluable. Such information is usually up-to-date and industry-specific and usually provides a very good source for checking out the competition and their products. This type of information is frequently biased by opinion and not altogether reliable in quantitative terms, but it often provides valuable subjective qualitative opinion.

The European Commission

The European Commission in Brussels is a good source of technical data. EC offices in major cities provide booklets on diverse subjects at a relatively low cost.

Chambers of commerce and EC trade associations

Information from this type of organisation's library will be made available to you if you contact your local representative.

The media

The media can provide very good factual and subjective information and updates. Especially effective are the *Financial Times* and the *Economist*.

Trade publications

Trade publications from around Europe often include a certain amount of statistical data. It is always worth seeing who is advertising from within your own trade. This may give some guide to competitor strategies.

Annual reports

Annual reports of competitors and potential customers may not always contain the same standard and type of information that is expected in the UK, but they are worth consulting nevertheless.

Promotional material

Competitors' catalogues and promotional material provide a good source for finding out what your competitors' strengths are.

Advertising agencies

Advertising agencies have access to media spend figures throughout the EC, and indeed the world. They, too, are well worth investigating.

Market research reports

Market research reports on specific industries, countries and products are published by many organisations such as Mintel, Jordans and Euromonitor.

BSI

The British Standards Institution are the best source of assistance with technical standards, and its technical help to exporters division gives specific assistance regarding technical information relating to standards and certification procedures in member states. They also provide assistance with regard to exhibitions, trade fairs, export documentation and insurance.

Employers' organisations

Organisations such as the CBI and the Institute of Directors can give extensive help in the area of export services. They produce much useful literature such as this CBI Initiative 1992 series.

Other sources

- Information on individual member states is often available from embassies or by visiting the relevant trade department within that member state.

- Banks are a particularly good source of information on countries and markets. Most major banks have international client networks and in some cases specialist divisions to further client services.

- Your *existing sales staff*, especially if they have a presence in the EC, are a source of high-quality information which is often overlooked.

Problem areas

Information gathering in a non-domestic market has some obvious pitfalls. The most obvious of these are discussed below.

Language

The first major problem to be encountered may be the language in which the information is presented. This is demonstrated in the often quoted example of the launch in China of the Pepsi slogan 'Come alive with Pepsi'. After market testing it was discovered that the slogan had been translated as 'Pepsi reawakens your dead relatives'. This is an exceptional example, but it shows that the problem can be one of basic translation and not necessarily of a technical nature.

In the early stages of assimilating market intelligence, however, the most frequent difficulty is that of obtaining accurate, useful, and technical translations. It is not enough to pass important competitor or market information to a distant relative who happens to have studied Spanish or German some years earlier as part of a degree course. To appreciate the nuances of emphasis and to avoid being misled by inaccurate translation, it is vital to employ the services of a professional, reputable translation agency. If possible, try to obtain details of translators who have a knowledge of your industry, as they will almost certainly be able to extract more information than an uninformed translator, no matter how proficient in languages. Larger companies, and those committed to long-term non-domestic marketing, will seek to employ a range of such skills in-house. While it is unlikely that resources will stretch to employing competent linguists for every market addressed, prioritisation can ensure that a high percentage of a company's targeted market place is covered by two, or at the most three, language skills. If resources are restricted, consideration should be given to hiring a receptionist with language skills – confusion and embarrassment (perhaps even lost sales) can arise from a lack of a basic working knowledge of customers' languages.

By and large the UK lags far behind its EC counterparts in language skills and a substantial market is now developing in short-term language training, and courses are now available to meet most companies' requirements. They are often run by chambers of commerce and local technical colleges.

Translators

Culture

Cultural values differ from member state to member state. The differences may be of a religious, ethical, social or traditional nature, and it is vital to get a sound understanding of the cultural nuances of each member state with which you wish to trade. Each national business community reflects its cultural environment, leading to widely different attitudes and practices. Doing business with a foreign colleague demands an understanding of these variations – what is acceptable behaviour in one context is not necessarily so in another.

While there are many excellent books (usually travel guides) which attempt to give an indication of the cultural differences that will be met (particularly in doing business from country to country in

Europe), it has to be accepted that it is almost impossible to gain a working understanding of cultural nuance without spending time in the country itself. Local contacts are an invaluable aid to reaching an understanding of cultural perceptions and it is absolutely vital that any significant meetings with potential customers, competitors, or indeed local colleagues, are subjected to a dry run with informed local advice, in order to avoid cultural *faux pas*.

The commitment to understanding cultural differences must also be made by senior management. A sales or marketing manager trying to explain to an unsympathetic marketing director that, for example, the offer of a working breakfast will not be welcomed in his territory, only to be over-ruled in the interests of 'getting the job done', will result not only in the possibility of lost sales but also in a downgrading of the company's reputation for genuine commitment to the local market.

It is, therefore, vital to ensure that any company's quality assurance techniques and procedures apply to the company's cultural interaction with the indigenous community. It should be part of any market entry strategy to ensure that the cross-functional teams mentioned in Chapter 13 contain at least one member with a considerable knowledge of local custom and practice. This team member may take the lead in establishing meetings, setting the tone of correspondence and deciding how best to respond to competitor/supplier/customer requests, even though a more senior team member may well decide upon the content of such responses.

Statistics

The availability of statistics on almost any product or industry on a national and an EC-wide basis is now so large as to be almost bewildering. Information gathering, particularly for the purposes of devising market entry strategies, seems destined to become statistics-driven. Comparisons of consumption patterns from member state to member state and historical and projected sales and market shares provide valuable documentation for any pan-European organisation. Nevertheless, the need to be fully aware of the assumptions under which statistics have been collated, always a major problem in any market, becomes absolutely crucial in dealing with statistics which relate to more than one market.

The following factors must be taken into consideration when gathering statistical information from different EC member states for market or other comparisons:

- The information, if it covers more than one member state, may well have been accumulated using different techniques, and over differing time frames

- The base measure of comparison may not be standard, even with sets of figures from the same member state due to currency fluctuations, for example

Consumption patterns

Consumption patterns require a careful, in-depth analysis. Take drug-prescribing for example: when researching the use of a particular drug in different member states, it may appear on the surface that usage in member state A is much lower than in member state B. However, analysis might show that doctors in member state A typically prescribe lower dose levels, using the drug in conjunction with one or more other drugs at the same time. This is a typical example of local preference (and a natural barrier). Similarly, any study of the extent of car ownership in, say, two member states may be distorted firstly by the degree of leasing and secondly by the fact that in somewhere like Britain some 70 per cent of car ownership is accounted for by company cars, whereas in Switzerland the incidence of company cars is much lower.

In the two examples above, any superficial analysis of drug usage or car ownership from member state to member state would yield significantly distorted results if the underlying assumptions were not taken into account. Adjustments may have to be made to take account of variations in consumption patterns before a true overall picture will emerge. To reduce the likelihood of coming to incorrect (and potentially dangerous) conclusions, your MIS should ensure that:

- Fundamental assumptions are not accepted until they have been subjected to independent review

- Information output is presented in a standardised format which compares like with like

- Statistics are not combined and aggregated where there is no justification for doing so

- Untested, dubious and material assumptions are listed on the face of any document containing inferences made from such assumptions

Information on public procurement

To realise the potential benefits from the opening up of the internal market for public procurement, businesses must not only have the right to bid across boundaries, they must also have *information* about the opportunities. The Commission must enforce the rights *and* ensure that the opportunities are widely publicised.

The OJ

In a perfect system, all public procurement contracts which exceed the minimum stipulated values, will be advertised in the OJ. Potential suppliers will then respond using the different approved types of procedure. Whether the advertising of notices in this way will be adequate remains to be seen. Few contracts, it is anticipated, will rely solely on the OJ publication for dissemination.

No Commission action is in any way a substitute for your own market assessment. Most businesses which have an interest in increasing their activity in a member state other than their home state, will undertake some or all of the preparatory investigations detailed in this chapter.

The basic Commission source of information on public procurement contracts is the OJ. The new directives on works and supplies, and the expected strengthening of the enforcement mechanisms, will serve to increase the amount of information on each contract and the assurance that it will be published. The usual contract notice will be summarised in each main EC language and a fuller statement, of up to 650 words, will be published in the language of the contract. This limit does not apply in the 'common position' on the Utilities Directive, although it is in the Supplies and Works Directive as amended. Further information will be supplied to enquirers.

TED

The Commission have made the notices available through TED (see p. 108), which is updated daily. TED is an online source of the information in the OJ. TED also includes notices for contracts in the African, Caribbean and Pacific countries linked to the EC (partly because of the requirements when they use development funds from the EC) as well as a number of Japanese contracts. Further discussions, at the time of writing, are taking place to consider the addition of contract notices from EFTA, Canada and the USA. Contracts coming under the GATT code are also published here. Since early in 1989, TED has also been used to publish the names of companies which have been awarded contracts.

The number of official contract notices will exceed 20,000 each year. You will usually only be interested in a small percentage of these and TED can be used selectively to provide you only with the information required. Tender notices are classified according to the four-digit NACE code used for industrial classifications in the EC. A user can therefore refine a request for information by the type of product and the country originating the notice. These services involve a user charge as well as the cost of the basic modem and terminal or telex machine. The cost entails both the telephone time and a cost of access to the database.

The TED database, and others, is operated by the European Communities Host Organisation (ECHO) (see p. 47).

Supplementary sources

Businesses wanting to make other enquiries about public procurement in member states may wish to approach the originating agencies direct. There is no complete or standard reference for this purpose, however, a list of relevant agencies is given in the annexes to the GATT agreement on government procurement, as an annex to the Supplies Directive, as Appendices 1 and 2 to the European Documentation pamphlet 'Public procurement and construction; towards an integrated market', and as annexes to the draft Directive for the 'excluded sectors'.

Sub-contracting

Greater knowledge of contract opportunities, and increased knowledge of the outcome of award procedures, opens up a new and extensive source of information of potential to sub-contractors and subsidiary suppliers. The name and location of a successful main contractor is a useful starting point for many small sub-contractors. So also is the procedure which asks works contracts to identify the probable areas and amounts of sub-contracting when a tender notice is published. A recent development which will facilitate this process is the publication through TED of the names of companies which have been awarded contracts. This will help sub-contractors take advantage of the opening of the market to the larger main contractors or suppliers.

Structural funds

All contracts funded from structural funds (Regional, Social and Agricultural Guarantee Funds, for example) and the European Investment Bank must observe the public procurement regulations. This means that the details of the allocation of such funds should be carefully watched: they provide an indication of likely sources of major contracts.

15. Market entry – gaining access

It is already generally accepted that the 1992 programme will bring about a fundamental review of the basic business strategies of most European businesses. The aspects of business strategy which require the most far-reaching review depend upon the company's current position in the EC market. Companies can be one of four types:

1. Based in the EC, trading in only one national market
2. Based in the EC, and already operating in most member states
3. Non-EC based with little or no market position in the EC
4. Non-EC based with a strong predominant market position in the EC.

In this chapter we will be focusing on companies in categories 1 and 3. Such companies will undoubtedly focus much of their business review on the area of market entry, in deciding whether or not to capitalise on the increased access to new markets. First of all, some points to watch out for in assessing market sectors and sizes will be outlined, followed by a review of the major market entry strategies available to such companies and concluding with a review of the importance on holding ground in the home market while exploring market entry abroad.

Assessing market sectors and sizes

The obvious first step in devising a market entry strategy is to use the information gathered (see Chapter 14) to reach initial conclusions regarding the size and type of the markets available. Such an analysis should involve five important elements: viability criteria, measurement criteria, market prioritisation criteria, a competitor profile and a market profile.

Viability criteria

Each organisation will have its own criteria by which it judges viability. These should be clearly stated in whichever terms the company's overall business strategy demands – the return on capital employed, increases in real added value, gross margins, net profit before tax, percentage market share – all of these and more can be used. The important point is that considered criteria are clearly established at the outset of the market sizing activity. In later stages it is all too easy, if such yardsticks have not been established, to take an optimistic view in the assessment of market sizes.

Measurement criteria

In establishing the size of the market sector, it is particularly important to ensure that the *real* market available to the company is being measured, not just the market which is *theoretically* available. Taking into account natural barriers to trade (local and regional purchasing patterns in particular) will dramatically reduce the size of the real market available to most companies for their products and services.

To return to the renowned French preference for top-loading washing machines, the unanalysed goods statistics show that on a 1988 basis the market in Europe for washing machines is 7 million per annum in total. Taken on its own, this is a considerable market sector in its own right. In reality, however, 95 per cent of washing machines sold in the UK market are front-loading, whereas 98 per cent of all washing machines sold in France are top-loaded. The French market accounts for almost 2 million units per annum. As a result a British manufacturer, geared up to produce only front-loading washing machines has a real market at least 2 million less than the perceived market. While this example is somewhat unsophisticated, and would (hopefully) be taken into account in any serious market analysis of the white goods sector, it none the less points out in stark terms the difference between measuring the real market and the perceived market.

Market prioritisation criteria

In order to establish an effective market entry strategy, relative weighting must be given to various factors to be considered in *prioritising* the various markets available. This will be a broader process than the establishment of *viability* in point one. The prioritisation of markets must take into account not only the market potential, but also the likely method of market entry (see p. 119), the desirability of the non-financial benefits of the market sector (status, competitor perception, key customer perception), and the opportunities to combine with other existing market sectors by product standardisation or modularisation.

Each company will ascribe differing relative importance to these and other prioritising factors and must develop such weighting indices by taking into account their own aims and ambitions. Again it is strongly recommended that such a process is completed *before* the assessment of market research is undertaken. The weighting should then be applied and rigorously examined. The temptation to leave such issues until after initial conclusions have been reached regarding the viability of various markets is a strong one, but leads to a generally over-optimistic application of such non-financial criteria.

Of course, it is open to any organisation to ignore the results of the application of market prioritisation criteria and to select potential markets on a more subjective basis, but the process outlined above will at least ensure that this is done in the light of an objective assessment and after consideration of potential markets on an equivalent basis. Reasons for derogation from the results of a market prioritisation appraisal should be documented for future review – the correctness or otherwise of the final decision may lead to a revision of the market prioritisation criteria.

Competitor profile

No assessment of any market sector can be considered complete without extensive analysis of competitors' weaknesses and strengths. It is probably not unfair to say that the largest omissions and most glaring departures from reality occur in this aspect of market assessment. Analysis of competitors should be thorough and realistic, covering not only their product and pricing strategies and current market position but also such items as their commitment to quality, reputation in the market place and perception of your company. Not only should *existing* competitors be examined but also *potential* competitors who may enter the market after 1992. Such an assessment should not be restricted to the merely objective. Subjective opinion can be very useful, depending on the source from which it is gleaned. In particular, the corporate culture of competitors is an important indicator as to the likelihood and extent of any response to your proposed new entry into the market place. Some estimate should be made not only of the points at which competitors are vulnerable (pricing, quality, labour, etc.) but also of the ways in which they are likely to respond, and where you are vulnerable.

One group of competitors not to be ignored are those which have *withdrawn* from the market for one reason or another. These are easy to miss, particularly if you are entering a market for the first time and are not aware of the history of product supply. The reasons for market withdrawal are often revealing, and may point to issues which will require to be addressed by your organisation if it is to maintain a mature position in the market place.

Market profile

Having considered all the matters above, a detailed market profile should be constructed for each potential new market, including all relevant information about the market place and the environment in which it operates. Each of the issues detailed above should be separately addressed and analysed in as standard a fashion as is possible, given the distortions from market to market.

Bear in mind that a market profile should contain much more than just marketing information. To provide a basis for decision making, the market profile should cover: marketing, fiscal matters, resource analysis, the legal environment, the political and economic environment and the impact and existence of technology.

Market entry strategies

Having analysed the various market sectors and sizes open to your company, the next step is to decide on the market entry strategy best suited to your organisation and the proposed market. This is a critical area of decision making as it will set in place the vehicle which will be used for trading in the new market place for many years to come.

There is no simple, universal, best strategy for gaining access to European markets. A company should consider all possible strategies for each individual market, country by country. The best strategy will be the one that satisfies the conflicting pressures of maximising existing domestic sales, while developing a European presence utilising the company's relative strengths in relation to the potential market.

For the smaller company, the immediate concern may be simply that of achieving critical mass within the single market, in order to survive in the era of increased competition post 1992. A multinational, on the other hand, may wish to take advantage of the opening up of markets to create a more homogeneous sales mix throughout the EC, diluting the percentage of domestic sales to the total and increasing the percentage of sales to the other non-domestic markets. A niche player may wish to be selective in the approach to new markets, perhaps even restricting selling to certain specified regions or cities which match its niche profile. As we have seen earlier, sellers of large capital goods may find their market entry programme developed for them by the movements towards consolidation in their customer industries. Third country suppliers, particularly in car manufacturing, financial services and assembly are currently taking a very diffuse approach to market entry, hurrying to locate in as many individual markets as possible.

Consequently it is clearly impossible to dictate any standard format for devising market entry strategy. It will be necessary for each company to review painstakingly each of the alternatives available for each market opportunity and to select those which have the best fit. The main options available are as follows.

Consolidate the domestic market

It must be borne in mind that there is no absolute imperative forcing companies to trade across national boundaries post 1992. Indeed it is probably fair to say that for the statistical majority of trading entities, the 1992 programme will not bring about a marked rise in export activity. Many thousands of small companies and owner-managed businesses will continue to supply their domestic market place – some with very parochial horizons, dictated by market opportunity and resource. For some companies, the pressure which exporting would place on management and resource will mean that there is no question of selling across national boundaries. For these companies, the main option is to consolidate at home and ensure that incoming competition is rebuffed.

Sell to a larger pan-European company

There is much merger and acquisition activity currently being undertaken throughout the EC. Mergers and acquisitions are the most common market entry technique now being employed. But for every acquirer there is an acquiree. For some companies the prospect of the post-1992 trading environment may seem grim, with the erosion of margins and the incursion of new competition into an already tight domestic market place. Many companies facing such a scenario will not have the management strength or depth of resources available to survive. The most prescient (or realistic) of these companies may recognise the impending threat and secure some form of continued trade by selling out to a dominant competitor. This is obviously a quick and easy way to obtain wide market access to the acquirers' markets, but it does usually lead to a loss of identity.

Mergers and acquisitions

As detailed above, mergers and acquisitions are currently the most favoured market entry strategy being pursued in the EC. An effective merger or acquisition can give immediate market access, strengthen management, and provide more resources to protect domestic markets. It has the added advantage of subsuming a competitor at the

Distribution
same time. For many companies the most difficult factor to address in contemplating market entry is that of distribution, and the acquisition of a company with existing distribution networks can be an immensely valuable combination, producing immediate added value.

Public procurement
In the field of public procurement, merger activity has been quiet until now. However, as the markets are opened up to non-national suppliers, it is anticipated that mergers and acquisitions will begin to take place in industries which supply a large part of their output to the public sector, such as the construction industry. These mergers will be mostly defensive – protecting local markets rather than entering new ones.

Strategic alliances

Strategic alliances cover a wide range of options, all of which are designed to allow two or more companies to combine in a market they might otherwise be unable to exploit. The component parts of a strategic alliance will take the form of some combination of joint venture, manufacturing under licence, agency-based distribution agreements and research and development (R&D) sharing. The Commission is particularly enthusiastic in promoting R&D joint venturing, and a number of EC-initiated multi-company programmes such as ESPRIT and JESSI exist, particularly in the computer and electronics field. These are discussed in more detail in later chapters.

Successful alliances
Success in strategic alliances, particularly joint venturing, is heavily dependent on early agreement of mutual ambitions and a clear statement of what is expected from each company. An unplanned, unmonitored, vague agreement to joint venture with 'an old colleague who happens to know the German market very well', set up by the Chairman after a long lunch, is unlikely to assist the company in obtaining its long-term objectives and may even result in an expensive drain on management time.

Joint ventures   Joint ventures are particularly suited to markets where majority outside share-holding is restricted or barred. Correctly initiated, they reduce the amount of foreign investment required by each individual party and bring together local market knowledge with manufacturing and distribution skills. As was seen earlier such an approach is likely where transportation or stock-holding costs prevent a company from servicing the European market excusively from a single manufacturing plant. Manufacturing under licence provides the necessary flexibility in adjusting for fluctuations in demand and thus overcoming the cost disadvantage.

Home-based sales team

This is the least expensive of all options but suffers the lack of flexibility and commitment to foreign markets which is required in a competitive environment. It is, however, particularly well suited to companies which have a limited number of large customers and where product servicing can be undertaken at a local level by some form of agency agreement. Large capital goods manufacturers and suppliers of raw materials and commodities may well continue to operate in this manner. Further reference to this type of market entry (and some others) will be made in the chapter on sales strategies.

Branch offices, subsidiary companies, green-field operations

This grouping of options gives the company the greatest degree of control over its activities in the non-domestic market. It brings with it a number of advantages:

- Profitability is not shared with any other party

- Quality and regularity of production can be more readily assured

- All personnel are accountable to the company

- The company is perceived as being committed to the local market

The disadvantages of such an approach can however, often outweigh the advantages. These include:

- High capital cost

- Recruitment and training issues

- Local fiscal, political and economic risks

All of these factors will be taken into account in the market profiling process detailed above and should be critically studied before selecting what to many companies will seem to be the natural method of market entry.

Holding on at home

As can be seen, there is a wide range of potential market entry strategies available to any company intending to sell outside of their domestic market. The correct selection of market entry strategy is vital for the long-term success of the company. In anticipating the use of any of the above strategies, care must be taken to ensure that the company does not lose sight of its overall corporate objectives.

An ambitious company will by its nature concentrate its activities on ensuring long-term growth. It is, therefore, natural for such an organisation to spend considerable resources on developing and implementing appropriate market entry strategies for the post-1992 single market. There is, however, only so much marketing resource available to any one organisation, and it is imperative to realise that every company's domestic market is another company's new entry opportunity. While you are planning market entry strategies to break into non-domestic markets, foreign companies are planning market entry strategies to break into your domestic market. As a result, one of the most important activities to be undertaken concomitantly with new market development is the maintenance and extension of your domestic market share.

Market share Companies will face competition in the domestic market from a number of sources:

- *Existing domestic competitors* who will see your expansion activities as an opportunity to renew their competitive challenge to your existing customer base

- *Incoming EC companies* setting up in your domestic market to exploit the new access available after 1992

- *Third country companies* establishing in your domestic market to protect against a 'Fortress Europe' policy

- *New companies* arising from the merger of EC organisations seeking to establish market dominance

In response to these threats to the domestic market, companies must move to protect their established customer loyalties and defend market share. There are two basic actions which must be undertaken by a company wishing to maintain or develop market share of its domestic base-developing defensive strategies and neutralising newcomers.

Develop defensive strategies

It is important to see that the essence of good defensive strategy is in many respects the other side of the coin to those activities undertaken in developing a market entry strategy. A strong defensive strategy, once developed, should result in any competitor who makes a market entry study of your domestic market coming to the conclusion that market entry is not viable. In other words, the best means of defence is to *avoid* the need for a head-to-head fight on your domestic market; it is much better to be in a position to discourage competitors from entering your market in the first instance. None the less, circumstances may occur where a company has to defend its market share against a new entrant.

Speedy retaliation   It is generally agreed that direct retaliation to a new entrant is one of the most efficient methods of deterring long-term commitment to the market place. The longer you wait to respond to market changes brought about by the new incoming competitor, the more entrenched his position will be and the deeper the roots formed in his supply cycle. It is important that any product changes or market innovations by the competitor should be met as soon as possible with generic product look-alikes. Additionally, competitive retaliation should be as specific as possible to the impact the new entrant is having on the market place. For example, price cuts, if necessary, should be restricted to commonly shared clients rather than extended to the total market, if at all possible. In this way defence costs (lost profits) are kept to a minimum and the likelihood of starting an all out competitive battle across the market is minimised.

Another way of deterring new entrants to your domestic market is to deny them any sense that their position within that market is stable. If you can reduce their returns to below those anticipated and ensure that position is maintained (at least in the competitor's perception) indefinitely, then eventual withdrawal is probable. As with any well planned company, the new entrant will have some market share and return on investment criteria by which viability is being measured, and prolonged denial of those returns will eventually cause shrinkage and perhaps eventually complete withdrawal. Unfortunately such an exercise is expensive for the defending company, involving reduction in margins and investment in new product development, perhaps far beyond usual time horizons. Selling vigorously into the market place to ensure a glut of supply can temporarily cause haemorrhaging in the new entrant's sales pattern, but the effect on customer relationships and long-term production costs must be taken into account. Nevertheless, in the light of the long-term market maintenance some of these costs may be worth paying in the short term.

Neutralising newcomers

Some of the market entry strategies detailed earlier can be seen as having a defensive pay-off. Strategic mergers, acquisitions and alliances with existing competitors in non-domestic markets can in effect neutralise the merged, acquired or joint-ventured company's desire to enter your domestic market. In contemplating the use of strategic mergers, acquisitions or other forms of alliance as a defensive strategy, it is important to have an accurate estimate of the likelihood of a particular competitor entering your domestic market in the first place, and an accurate assessment of the financial impact.

It should be self-evident that many so called competitors within the industry are in fact no threat, due to distinct market segments which they serve, or other types of product differentiation. There may be little to be gained from seeking an alliance with such a 'competitor'. However, what if such a company were itself to merge or acquire another competitor with a similar product profile to your own? Would the combination of the two product portfolios leave you struggling to service customers who would see the newly merged competitor as a one-stop shop across the broad range of their needs? If that is the case, then your company should be considering co-operation with such 'non-competitors' to offer a threat of wide product portfolio to other possible inward investors.

Alternatively, there may be competitors who have a similar product range but who are geographically weak where you are strong and vice versa. Aligning with such an organisation might provide the degree of market fit which would in effect provide an umbrella against incoming market competitors.

Commitment   Finally Michael E. Porter, in his definitive *Competitive Strategy* (Macmillan, 1980) points out that perhaps the single most important concept in planning a defensive competitive move is the concept of *commitment.* Perceived commitment to retaliating to offensive moves by competitors, commitment that the firm is unequivocally sticking with any moves it is making, commitment that the firm is intent in carrying out its strategy, is in the last analysis the most convincing method of communicating to a competitor that your domestic market is not up for grabs.

16.   Maintaining competitive advantage

Having gathered and structured the available market information, analysed the market sectors and sizes, produced a strategic marketing plan which includes market entry strategies, and developed the organisational structures necessary to manage the marketing process; having successfully implemented those plans and having achieved a substantial presence in new European markets, the company will want to maintain and develop that position for the foreseeable future. The ability of a company to maintain and develop its European market spread will depend to a great extent on its competitive advantages.

In this chapter, we will discuss competitive advantage, its development within a company, and the impact of competitor strategies. We will then look at how the market place itself can yield competitive advantage to a particular company and what role the industry as a whole plays in assisting in the process of identifying and maximising competitive advantage. Finally, we will review the use of competitive advantage in meeting market pressure from competitors, buyers and suppliers.

Competitive advantage

Competitive advantage is any advantage specific to a company which provides it with an edge over its competitors in the market place. It must, of course, come from the perceived value of a company's products or services to its customer base or potential customer base. Competitive advantage is not arrived at internally, nor is it something bestowed upon a company by its peers. Competitive advantage is only proved when its existence is acknowledged by the buyer. The two most frequent sources of competitive advantage will therefore be:

- Cost leadership
- Product differentiation (uniqueness)

A competitive advantage can also arise from idiosyncratic factors inherent in the nature of the market place or of the industry of which the company is a part. Each of these is examined in more detail below.

The ultimate aim in developing a strategy on the basis of competitive advantage is to be able to control (or at least react favourably to):

- The entry of new competitors to the market place

- The threat of substitutes

- The bargaining power of buyers

- The bargaining power of suppliers

- Rival actions of existing competitors

The effect of these factors on a company varies from industry to industry and, in an evolving market, the possible permutations and cumulative effect of each of these five external pressures requires that the company's competitive advantage be regularly reviewed and its existence confirmed and maintained, and improved, if possible. Some of the ways in which competitive advantage can be used to meet the five threats detailed above are explored in the final section in this chapter.

Competitive advantage in the company

Cost leadership

This source of competitive advantage is most common in a high volume production environment, where severe cost and overhead control, ruthless elimination of ancillary activities and efficient account management are brought to focus on the achieving of maximum returns from minimum inputs. Achieving higher than average returns in any particular industry obviously puts the company in a strong defensive position. Potential new entrants will need to spend a high proportion of their profits on advertising and promotion either above or below the line, and including product discounts. The company with a cost leadership will be able to withstand such a strategy for a prolonged period of time.

It should not be imagined, however, that cost advantages can be maintained in the long term at the expense of quality and service. Absolute reduction of costs, at the expense of perceived quality, will result in a value for money decision by the buyer, which will in effect erode or remove the perceived leadership. Cost leadership must therefore be seen to be different from lowest cost, and includes the meeting of customers' needs for value for money. Companies known to have emphasised a cost leadership strategy included Texas Instruments and Black and Decker.

An interesting – if risky – use of cost leadership strategy is to implement it in industries which have traditionally not used such a yardstick in measuring customer satisfaction. Amstrad attempted to do this in the PC market. Of particular interest was the response of those competitors who had not perceived cost leadership as an advantage in the computer industry.

Product differentiation

To develop a product or service that is perceived throughout the industry as being unique is every marketeer's dream. Differentiation can occur in many ways:

- In the quality of customer service

- In the geographical coverage of outlets

- In the inherent technology

- In available customisation

- In design

- In brand image

The Apple Macintosh computer, McDonald's fast food restaurants, Marriott Hotels, Short Brothers' 360 turbo-prop, the Anglepoise lamp, are all examples of products or services which have established a competitive advantage as a result of differentiation. In every case, the product or service development was specifically geared to the market niche and to the demands of the customer. It would be impossible to envisage any of these or similar products emerging from a production- or finance-led organisation. The emphasis towards customer satisfaction is almost always evident in companies whose cost advantage is differentiation.

Unlike cost leadership, product differentiation is generally not associated with high sales volumes and may, on occasion, be mutually exclusive of obtaining a large market share. Differentiation often requires an aura of exclusivity. Certainly, differentiation is generally at odds with cost leadership in terms of the high degree of spend in

R&D, product design, detailed customer support in infrastructure and high quality materials.

A company which has differentiation as its competitive advantage, and which has been accustomed to selling into its domestic market, will almost certainly address the wider European market at first by means of a home-based sales team. This is because of the need to control costs and the ability of the product to 'sell itself' if it does have a high degree of exclusivity.

On the other hand, companies with cost leadership advantage may well attempt market entry in Europe through some form of joint venture, perhaps manufacturing under licence in order to obtain low transportation and stockholding costs, and perhaps to reduce operating expenses by using a lower waged economy. This is discussed further on pp. 133–4.

Understanding competitor strategies

Our earlier definition of competitive advantage established that its existence must give the company an edge over its competitors. If such an edge does not exist, the competitive advantage is illusory. The ultimate arbiter as to the existence of the advantage, is the customer. Competitive advantage must clearly, therefore, be sustainable, not only against competitors' current activities, but also against their intended strategies.

Maintaining, reinforcing or improving competitive advantage is a process which must be constantly under review, and the primary impetus for such a review will be an analysis of competitors' strategies. With a competitor analysis, as was discussed earlier, it is imperative that not only are *existing competitors* scrutinised, but also that *potential competitors* are anticipated and some estimate of their future strategy arrived at.

New competitors   Attempting to forecast the entry of new competitors is never an easy task, but reviewing the analyses recommended in earlier chapters regarding market entry and holding on at home, the following potential sources of new competitors should be reviewed:

- New entities arising out of mergers and acquisitions

- Companies in your supply-chain (buyers or sellers) who may decide to integrate vertically into your market

- Other EC-based companies not yet trading in your newly acquired market

- Third country companies seeking to establish a base, either specifically in your target market, or in Europe generally.

Having established the existing and potential competitors, the next step is to subject their strategy to a detailed diagnosis. There are a number of classical theories on the component parts of a competitor analysis, most of which are a version of the traditional SWOT analysis (strengths, weaknesses, opportunity and threats). Whatever format you prefer, the analysis should cover the following key points.

History

This is often the only review made of competitors – an analysis of their past and current financial performance, covering market share, market place perception, successes and failures and reaction to changes in the market place in the past. Such an analysis is, however, only the initial stage of building a profile leading to an assessment of the competitor's likely future strategy.

Current position and strategy

A competitor's operating strategy can generally be readily adduced from its current activities and competitive interaction. Current market intelligence, supplier and customer information and reaction to specific market changes will all give indications of the competitor's current strategy towards your market place.

Strengths and weaknesses

A review of competitive strengths and weaknesses will by its nature be a combination of subjective and objective information, covering such areas as its management and organisation, finance and resource, research and development skills, product portfolio and perception, marketing, selling and operational skills and the extent of its distribution network (if relevant). These and other matters should be examined with a view to establishing:

- What the company perceives as its own strengths
- What the company's real strengths are
- What the company perceives as its real weaknesses
- What the company's real weaknesses are

Probable ambitions

Some estimate of the competitor's probable future ambitions will give an indication of what strategy is required to move the competitor from its existing position (analysed above) to its required position. This should not just cover the area of financial return, but should cover such items as market share, the involvement of technology, commitment to the environment and overall strategic requirements. Obtaining indications of probable future ambitions is not easy, and will involve consideration of many aspects of the competitor's activities, including:

- Ultimate ownership

- Organisational structure

- Management ambitions

- Management style

- Corporate ethos

- Interaction with parent, subsidiary, associated companies

- Original reason for market entry

- Strategic importance of market to overall strategy

- Overall goals of ultimate owner

- Likely required financial returns

- Approaching legislative, economic or political changes material to the competitor

Analysis of competitors

Detailed analyses of competitors, covering each of the areas detailed above, will provide a firm basis on which to make assumptions regarding competitor strategies. While such assumptions must, by their nature, be to some extent subjective, it should be possible to predict with a degree of certainty, the competitor's basic stance towards your competitive advantage and any changes that may occur in the market place, whether offensive or defensive. It is worth producing an analysis on the competitor's ability to act in each of these directions: is the competitor largely satisfied with its current position, and basically attempting to defend its market share, or is it dissatisfied and likely to move to an offensive stance to increase market share?

Later in this chapter, we will consider the use of competitive advantage as a defence against competitor strategies.

Competitive advantage in the market place

Some elements of competitive advantage can accrue from the market place itself, rather than from the individual company. It should be clear that such advantages are conceptual only until appropriated by a particular company, and that the competitive advantage to that company exists by nature of its location (or use of) the market place, but unlike company-based advantages (cost leadership or differentiation) market place competitive advantage cannot be defended exclusively by any one company; other companies may enter the market place and similarly exploit its indigenous competitive advantages. Some of the **Types of advantage** types of competitive advantage inherent in market place locality include:

- *Labour costs* – One of the most common causes of the attraction of heavy industry is the existence of a low-wage economy. Many shoe manufacturers located their production facilities in Portugal for this very reason. It should, however, be noted that labour costs savings can often be relative – many of the relocated shoe manufacturers found that the indigenous Portuguese shoe companies had moved their production facilities to Morocco to obtain even cheaper wage rates!

- *Proximity to raw materials* – A production process which uses, for example, large amounts of water, may find that its costs can be dramatically cut by locating close to large sources of water. Similar factors apply to other necessary commodities.

- *Marketing economies of scale* – High demographic density over a relatively small area can produce marketing economies of scale which would otherwise be lost over a wider area with a less dense population. Shorter, more intense sales trips, supply networks and maintenance costs will accrue. The evolving concept of the European 'magic triangle' and the so-called 'global highway' are all based around the ability to reach the largest amount of customers in the smallest area, at the lowest cost.

- *Purchasing advantages* – Locating in a market place which contains a substantial number of material suppliers, brings with it the (somewhat non-quantifiable) ability to develop a strong supply-chain relationship and to develop barriers to entry for competitors by conferring most favoured supplier status. Although it would be most unusual for this to be the primary reason for location in a particular market place, it can have a substantial secondary effect.

- *Access to technology* – Increasingly, the availability of communications and technology facilities will be a deciding factor in location of activity. The Republic of Ireland is a good example of a market place which, realising its inefficiencies in global telecommunications, invested heavily in restructuring its communications industry and re-equipped for growth. As a result, the Customs House development in Dublin has become a successful market leader in front office financial services activity, with many world leaders in the industry locating there.

Competitive advantage in the industry

Competitive advantage can also be gained from the company's position within its industry. In this context Michael Porter (*Competitive Strategy*) identifies five broad industry environments:

- Fragmented industries

- Emerging industries

- Mature industries

- Declining industries

- Global industries

Relating each of these to their likely position in the post-1992 single market may give some indication of the nature of likely competitive advantage within those industries in the new environment.

Fragmented industries

A detailed analysis of fragmented industries was carried out in Chapter 11 using the grid process to differentiate between those industries fragmented by artificial barriers to trade, and those which will have continuing natural barriers to trade. As shown there, the degree of restructuring post-1992 will depend on the interaction between artificial and natural barriers to trade. The grid will help you to track the effects of the 1992 programme on your own company.

Competitive advantage is likely to accrue to companies and fragmented industries which are actively involved in lobbying and tracking legislative and other changes which will result in consolidation of their industry. Companies undertaking strategic mergers, acquisitions, and other alliances to bind their market place together, will emerge in 1993 ahead of the pack.

Emerging industries

Companies in emerging industries tend to be sharply defined as either pioneer innovators, or 'me-too imitators'. Consequently, competitor relationships can tend to be particularly brittle with pride at stake to an even larger degree than in established industries. Typically, the pioneer innovator will invest too much money in attempting to defend the indefensible – a monopolistic approach to market share based on their view that they discovered the market in the first place and it therefore belongs wholly to them. Me-too imitators, on the other hand, tend to have a short shelf-life, often set up with inadequate resourcing, hoping to capitalise on a swiftly expanding market, and achieving volume sales. With the advent of the single market of 323 million people, and very few artificial barriers to trade (new industries tend not to have deep-seated differences in standards and practices), the advantage will tend to lie with the me-too imitator, which can capitalise on the pioneer's R&D expenditure, produce cheaper, substitute products and sell them into the larger market. Typically, the pioneer innovator will have sold only into his domestic market, trying to maintain product quality and constantly refining and customising the product. As a result, the pioneer innovator will have no distribution or supply cycle in the rest of the EC and will be consequently vulnerable.

Mature industries

Companies in non-fragmented mature industries are already operating in an environment where the scramble for increased market share has become more pronounced as a result of slower growth, leading to an increased emphasis on quality of service, lower costs and an expected excellence in all aspects of manufacture, marketing, selling and distributing. In a mature market, product innovation and new product development will, by definition, be slower and less frequent and, overall, industry profits will tend to be in decline.

As a result, most companies in mature industries will already have been looking outside their domestic market to increase turnover and profitability, and competitive advantage will accrue to those companies which have already established strong relationships in other member states. In particular, companies which can aggressively sell existing products into new markets, thus taking up excess capacity in existing production facilities, will have a considerable advantage over competitors who wrongly over-emphasise the need for new products to boost sales.

Declining industries

Declining industries have already been discussed in the context of public procurement, where there are a number of industries which have an excessive percentage of their output bought by the public sector, and which are in decline as a result of reduced public sector demand. Examples of such industries include the boiler manufacturing industry, which is heavily dominated by a few small companies, and in France, the steel industry, which has been severely cut back and has seen the merger of the two largest state-owned companies, Usinor and Sacilor. Competitive advantage in a declining market after 1992 will fall to the company which can do one of the following:

- Dominate the European market place

- Spin off a niche market which is profitable and perhaps expanding

- Liquidate all or part of the business and reinvest elsewhere

Global industries

Companies trading in industries which are already multi-national by nature will experience increased commercial pressures post-1992 arising from the following:

- Inward investment by third country competitors, largely from the USA and Japan, locating in Europe ahead of the completion of the single market, to obtain a bridge head in 'Fortress Europe'

- The potential disturbance of relationships with governments in European markets. Protected national champions and overall public procurement will be dramatically altered by the changes detailed in Part I of this book. As a result, many multinationals will find their European sales mix will be substantially re-profiled

Competitive advantage may accrue therefore to those multinationals which are not dependent on public sector sales to a large extent, and who are not competing with Japanese and US inward investments. EC-based multinationals which may have been in a position to treat Europe as a single market for some time, may now be profiling marketing activities outside the EC.

Using competitive advantage

Having identified the competitive advantages accruing to a company, either inherently in its activities, arising out of the market place in which it operates, or out of the industry of which it is part, it may be useful as a post-script to review how competitive advantage may be used to protect a company's position in the market place.

At the outset of this chapter, we listed the five main areas from which a company will experience pressure: the entry of new competitors, the threat of substitutes, the bargaining power of buyers, the bargaining power of suppliers, and the rival actions of existing competitors. The different ways in which cost leadership and product differentiation protect a company against these pressures, will give an insight into the competitive advantage best suited for your company in the light of its trading environment. Cost leadership will effectively protect a company against the five pressures by ensuring that the returns are higher than those earned by competitors, by preventing buyers from driving prices down much further, by giving a comfort zone against suppliers who insist on large cost increases, and by erecting barriers to entry for substitutes and competitors in terms of scale economies. Product differentiation on the other hand, protects companies by providing customer loyalty. This is the main barrier of entry to potential competitors, and the main reason for sympathetic action by buyers. The higher margins achieved through product differentiation gives a degree of strength in relationships with suppliers, and the very nature of product differentiation means that substitutes are not available.

Reviewing your position

Once a competitive advantage has been earned, care should be taken to review the company's position regularly (perhaps as part of the annual review process) to ensure the continued existence of the competitive advantage. It is unfortunately not uncommon to find a senior management which is still convinced that their company has a competitive advantage which was, in fact, lost some time ago, and exists only in their own minds. Such a review of competitive advantage should include industry and competitor analysis, together with a review of existing or potential advantages accruing from the market place itself.

Transferability   Finally, you should take care not to assume that competitive advantage will transfer across national boundaries. Competitive advantage in one country does not guarantee competitive advantage in another. Cost advantage will be distorted by local overhead structures and transportation and stock-holding costs. Product differentiation is harder to measure and the existence of natural barriers to trade may erode or eliminate what was originally viewed as a competitive advantage.

An example of this problem was encountered by the Northern Ireland-based animal hygiene company, Kilco Chemicals Ltd (see Appendix 6). Kilco produce a product called Lanodip, a teat dip to prevent mastitis in cows. The main selling point of this product in the UK was the inclusion of lanolin in its formulation. This gave the product a pleasing silkiness – a decided advantage for farmhands who might be applying the product at repeated intervals to large herds. The company marketed the product under the slogan 'Lanodip – the silky touch'. The product proved to be extremely popular with UK farmers, largely based on tactile acceptability. However, when Kilco tried to market the product in West Germany, one of the major problems encountered was the perception of lanolin as an ingredient in the formulation. The predominance of green issues in Germany at that time, together with agricultural perceptions, meant that Kilco were obliged to undergo comprehensive and frequent testing of their product, changing the formulation regularly, all of which delayed market entry for a period in excess of eighteen months. What had proved to be a real competitive advantage for Kilco in the UK proved to be a stumbling block to trade in Germany.

17. Product strategy

Product strategy is a vital element of any company's marketing mix. Product strategies fall into two categories, those for market entry, and those for market development. As we have seen, correctly targeting markets and devising entry strategies achieves little if the product to be sold is not suited to that market.

Market entry

In this chapter, we will look at the importance of market entry product strategies for companies wishing to sell their products to the public sector and industry in the EC. A brief survey will be made of the consequences of harmonisation of technical standards upon product strategies, and of the variety of product strategies available, including an analysis of the importance of new product development in the European context. In closing, the relevance of developing a product portfolio, particularly in international markets, is discussed.

This book is particularly concerned with marketing to the public sector and industry (broadly, business-to-business activities). Consequently, little coverage is given to product branding and packaging and their relation to consumer goods. The intention in this chapter is to indicate areas for further research and investigation, not to detail specific strategies which can be adopted wholesale.

Definitions

In order to ensure common purpose, it might be useful to define some of the more frequently used terms in this chapter, and to put them in the context of an overall marketing strategy.

Products (as defined here) includes both goods and services. The *total product* includes all the benefits received by a customer in the purchase transaction – both tangible and intangible. Two customers making the same purchase may acquire (or think they acquire) different benefits, and thus the total product concept can be used to *segment* the market a product reaches. There are obviously a wide range of *product development* options open to any seller, and combining development techniques with basic product *characteristics* (design, features, packaging, etc.) will result in a *product line* or *range*. Interacting with the marketing function, to ensure compatibility with the market place and the overall marketing strategy of the company, will result in a planned *product strategy*.

Derived demand

In the context of marketing to the public sector and industry (as opposed to selling to consumers in the retail market), it is important to note that industrial products all have one common attribute: they experience *derived demand*. In other words the demand for all industrial products depends ultimately on the demand for another product – that produced by your customer. The demand for aircraft seat belts depends upon the demand for aircraft. The demand for greasepaint depends upon the demand for theatre seats. (Tracing this through, the demand for any product depends ultimately on the demand from consumers for finished goods and services; there is no genuinely business-to-business activity that stands complete on its own.) Consequently it is always of importance to track your *customers' product strategies* as these will ultimately impact upon your own approach to product development and mix.

Harmonisation of technical standards

In Part II we reviewed the progress being made by the Commission and national governments in harmonising technical standards and the associated testing and certification procedures. In mature industries the variation in standards has produced an array of barriers to trading across national boundaries, often protecting national industries or responding to uniquely local concerns. The immense cost of such fragmentation is seen in the competitive price paid in many industries. It has been estimated, for example, that the USA spent approximately $3 billion developing the three main telephone switching systems in use, compared with an estimated $1.5 billion in Japan for one system. In Europe, on the other hand, the EC member states spent an aggregate of $10 billion developing ten systems to meet the differing national standards.

Removing such technical barriers to trade should result in an increase in competition across national boundaries as obvious anomalies such as that in the telecommunications industry are eventually harmonised. This process has two main implications for product strategies: higher standards and longer production runs.

Higher standards

The intentions of the Commission are to ensure that the quality of European standards should be no lower than the highest prevailing national standards. While this aim will certainly be diluted in the search for a compromise between the pressures arising from an exceptionally ambitious programme, national bodies lobbying for local preference, and the need to complete implementation in a relatively short time, it is clear that the general level of harmonised European standards will be very high.

This will produce benefits for those companies which already manufacture to high standards (and which, therefore, will not need to re-tool or re-design if higher European standards are adopted). Any company intending to compete across national boundaries in Europe should anticipate this trend by not restricting compliance with standards to those of the domestic market or the target market. If neither the domestic nor target markets have the highest industry standards, consideration should be given to upgrading the compliance process to those higher standards. Otherwise the process may need to be undertaken twice, often at considerable expense. This particularly applies to products which are in development stage, and are therefore in a position to be redesigned (where necessary) without expensive disruption to the manufacturing process.

Longer production runs

As the need to differentiate products to meet varying national standards disappears, companies with such products will have longer production runs, from which a number of national markets can be served, resulting in economies of scale. This is, of course, at the hub of the Commission's aspirations for the single market, and the basis of many of the calculations of potential benefits of the 1992 programme. The effect of continuing natural barriers to trade will dramatically reduce this benefit for many companies as they continue to require some degree of product differentiation, but such differentiation is likely to be in the area of product design and packaging, rather than inherent in engineering or component construction. As a result, the costs of differentiation should reduce, and the impact on stock-holdings marginalised. Indeed many companies may well choose to manufacture only standardised products, maximising economies of scale, and enter into licensing or other agreements with local companies to undertake customising for the local market as appropriate.

Product strategies for new markets

As was stated at the outset of the chapter, it is essential that the product strategy is compatible with the market in which the product is to be sold. It is consequently highly unlikely that the product strategy adopted in the domestic market will be appropriate for the new European markets into which you will wish to sell after 1992. However, companies intending to enter new markets, particularly those doing so for the first time, often restrict consideration of alternative product strategies to either minimum product adaption to meet the legislative requirements of the new market, or new product development – meeting the new market's needs from scratch. These options represent only the extremes of a wide range of revised product strategies available to the new market entrant, and indeed represent on the one hand the least satisfactory option for a market-led company (minimum adaption), and on the other the most expensive option (new product development).

The options   Some alternative options are briefly outlined below. Bear in mind that the best strategy to adopt will come out of the market entry process outlined in Chapter 15, and that the market profile for each member state may dictate a different approach from member state to member state, if you intend to sell to more than one new market.

Product differentiation

The differentiation of products to compensate for differing consumer preferences is the most obvious product strategy for new market entry and, as stated above, usually one of the earliest strategies to be considered by companies attempting to sell into new markets. Generally speaking, product differentiation tends to be restricted to the minimum necessary to meet additional or different legislation in the target market. It will be necessary for companies to recognise that the harmonisation of standards will not remove the requirement for product differentiation. As has been stated many times, natural preferences will still remain for many years in member states, and products will need to be altered to take these into account.

Product positioning

The market-led company will already have explored product positioning in its home market, stressing product characteristics (tangible or intangible) which ensure its attraction to a certain part of the market.

When contemplating a move into a new market, the product positioning strategy can often be positively reviewed on the existing product line, to produce an apparently 'new' product. In motor car distributorship, for example, the concept of the 'fleet car' varies somewhat from country to country, with a vehicle which in one country may be viewed as too downmarket for the executive fleet or too upmarket for the sales fleet, being quite acceptable in another country in both cases.

Product quality review

Allied to the concept of product positioning – where a product remains unchanged, but sells because it is perceived differently in different markets – is product quality review, where again the product remains fundamentally unchanged, but secondary characteristics such as the materials utilised are changed to take the product up or down the quality scale to fit a perceived gap in the target market. In the domestic market, demand may not exist at a certain quality level, or may be dominated by one or more competitors. The manufacture of rolling stock for railways is a good example of a product which on account of differing consumer preferences throughout the EC, requires supply at different levels of quality.

Quality creep   In implementing product quality review, it is important to guard against quality creep. This occurs when design or other adaptions are upgraded internally by successive 'improvements', leading ultimately to a product that has been upgraded beyond its natural selling point. Such a process will reduce, or eliminate the available market size. Adding quality beyond the point of economic return is most common in smaller, family companies, where quality is often a tradition and a point of pride, but some larger companies have had to suffer expensive product failures as a result of quality creep.

Product adaption

In the last example the secondary characteristics of a product were reviewed with the intention of moving the product up or down the quality scale. Product adaption involves altering some of the product's primary characteristics, resulting in an allied, but different, product.

An example of a successfully adapted product is the Sherpa military aircraft. Produced by Short Brothers of Belfast (now part of Bombardier, the Canadian transport manufacturer), the Sherpa began life as the Shorts 360, a turbo-prop commuter aircraft, commonly used by airlines for domestic short-distance flights. By altering the internal specification considerably, the product was successfully adapted to become the Sherpa, a military aircraft, now used throughout the world for training and troop transportation.

Product elimination

Adding, changing and repositioning products must be accompanied by a realistic review of products which will not sell in material amounts in the new targeted market. The market research outlined in earlier chapters will have led to an assessment of the market, which, accompanied by test marketing, will allow a reasonably objective analysis to be made of the likelihood of products selling. Products which are unlikely to yield an economic return, and which cannot be adapted or repositioned, must not be offered in the new market.

This is often one of the hardest decisions to be made in devising product strategy for new markets, particularly if those devising the strategy were involved in the success of the elimination candidate in the domestic market. It is a trait of many marketing managers to be optimistic in outlook, and some refuse to believe, despite all the evidence, that a successful domestic product will not sell in a new target market. There are two common mistakes made in this regard. The first is failure to discount the 'honeymoon effect' caused by bringing any new product into a market and basically results in an inflation in perceived demand in the test marketing phase. This is caused by a number of factors, one of which is a general interest in any new product by informed buyers, who wish to garner information; this general interest is not the same as buying interest, and is not in itself enough to maintain a market for the product. The second mistake is failing to eliminate the original product after it has undergone adaption or repositioning. Often out of pride, tradition or emotional attachment, the company finds it is unable to replace the old product entirely, and offers it to the new market anyway 'to see how it goes'. This will usually result in much reduced returns overall, as the old product yield dilutes that of the new. (There can be, and are, exceptions, where against all the indications, an old unadapted product outsells the new revised version, but these exceptions are rare, and generally only the largest companies have the resources available to take the risk.)

Product rejuvenation

Product elimination may have already occurred in the domestic market on products which, for one reason or another, did not sell in the volumes expected or necessary to obtain adequate returns. It is worthwhile investigating such products to ascertain the precise reason for the decision to eliminate them, looking in particular for products which could not attain high enough sales in the domestic market alone, but which could be sold in the larger European market at levels high enough to produce a satisfactory return, and for products which were not acceptable to the domestic customer, but which, adapted, repositioned (or not) will sell into another target market in the EC.

Product line extension

Every company has a product line – that is, the range of products it offers to the customer. The number of products in a product line may range from one to thousands, depending on the company. Each product strategy outlined in this section will affect the size of the company's total product range, as products are added, adapted, or eliminated.

It is, however, an important product strategy in itself to review the intended product range for each target market. The company which has successfully traded in the home market with only one product may find that, as a result of customer preferences, it must supply a wider choice to obtain market entry. The office stationery supplier, for example, who has established a firm reputation on a single type of paper clip, may find that (even to gain access to buyers) he must present a wider range of options. Alternatively, the domestic ambulance manufacturer, discussed in earlier chapters, may have successfully developed a wide range of product customisations for the home market. The best product strategy for market entry in a European target market may well be to concentrate on a smaller number of options, sold aggressively to one or two customers.

Product life-cycle review

The concept of the product life-cycle could legitimately take a chapter on its own, but in the context of market entry product strategies, should be seen as a useful variation of the repositioning strategy discussed earlier. Indeed the product life-cycle concept is best used as a planning tool at the point of market entry. In broad terms, products undergo a four-stage life-cycle, approximating to the Introductory, Growth, Maturity and Decline stages in the product's life. Profits earned by the product will peak at the Growth stage, before competition and reducing demand begin to dilute returns. By the time the

Decline stage occurs, the wise supplier will be keeping prices low, ready to liquidate stock when demand stalls, milking the product brand of any benefits available, and seeking alternative products to introduce to the product range at the Introductory level, where competition is minimal, and where, although profits aren't yet maximised, the company can begin to build customer loyalty – the basis for entering the Growth phase.

Although greatly simplified, it can be seen from this analysis of the product life-cycle that one of the most expensive errors in devising a market entry product strategy is to ignore or misinterpret the phase of the product life-cycle appropriate to the product and the new market. Different markets can be at different stages of a product's life cycle for many reasons, including, but not restricted to, customer preference. A consulting firm, for example, selling privatisation skills to the public sector will find a radically different phase of the product life-cycle from one member state to the next.

New product development (NPD)

In Chapters 11 and 16, the restructuring and consolidating effects of the 1992 programme were discussed. One of the results of such a process will undoubtedly be an increase in new product development as competitiveness increases across industries. However, for many companies, the development of totally new products from scratch should be the *last* market entry product strategy to be considered. It is expensive, time-consuming, and easy to get wrong. A market entry strategy needs to be timely, and should have a low risk profile (the costs of withdrawal from a market due to product failure can be immense, financially and otherwise), so it is best to adopt an alternative product strategy where possible. Exceptions are industries which already have large investments in R&D activity, such as electronics, pharmaceuticals and biotechnology, where the harmonisation of standards will increase the potential returns by opening up much wider markets, both at the component and final product level. Philips, for example, has estimated the cost of adapting television sets to meet the different technical standards in each EC member state at about $20 million per annum. The elimination of such costs will enable small, innovative companies to bring new products to the market, achieving economic returns previously not possible. In theory, testing and certification procedures should also be greatly reduced by harmonisation, reducing the time taken to bring a product to the market, and therefore increasing the attractiveness of NPD as a market entry product strategy.

EUREKA

In the R&D-intensive industries, there is much room for collaborative NPD, with quite a number of schemes available (many of them sponsored by the EC) to promote and fund development of generic R&D across industries. Around half of the Commission's research funding goes to commercial programmes, of which approximately $6 billion is allocated to programmes such as EUREKA. EUREKA is primarily focused on development (as opposed to basic research) in high-technology industries, and has as its aim the strengthening of such industries in Europe (including some non-EC countries) in competition with Japan and the USA. Each country has its own EUREKA secretariat and, to qualify for assistance, applications must be made by organisations from more than one EUREKA secretariat, thus guaranteeing a collaborative element. Other important collaborative frameworks are ESPRIT (European Strategic Programme for Research and Development in Information Technology) the key areas of which are advanced microelectronics, advanced information processing, software technology, office automation and computer-integrated manufacturing; BRITE (Basic Research in Industrial Technologies for Europe) which is mainly concerned with laser technology, assembly technology and CAD/CAM; and RACE (Research and Development in Advanced Communications Technology for Europe) which is mainly concerned with integrated high-speed telecommunications networks, integrated broadband communications. Similar, but more industry-focused programmes include AIM (Advanced Informatics in Medicine), DELTA (Development of European Learning Through Technological Advancement) and JESSI (Joint European Semiconductor Silicon Project).

For those companies in the sectors involved in highly intensive R&D, such programmes can provide an excellent funding and joint-venturing vehicle, with impressive added spin-offs in terms of publicity and end-product credibility. If you feel such programmes can be of assistance to you, the best starting point is the local DTI office. They will help you explore the options. They also produce a useful publication called 'A Guide to European Community Research and Development Programmes'.

Building a product portfolio

Product portfolio theory is an important adjunct to market entry product strategies. Notwithstanding the 1992 programme, selling into multiple markets increases exposure to many more political, economic and legislative variables than before, and thus heightens the risk of failure. Just as investors will spread resources across a number of investment vehicles to reduce the risk of exposure to the collapse of any one investment, so the product strategies detailed above should be implemented in a manner designed to ensure a spread of risk. There are many product portfolio models available, and a company seeking to build a strong product portfolio should ensure that the correct model is implemented to meet its specific needs, using outside consulting help, if necessary. Most portfolio models seek to spread products between those which have:

- A high market share in a high growth market

- A high market share in a low growth market

- A low market share in a high growth market

- A low market share in a low growth market

Products in the first category are the high yield products which tend to receive a lot of attention within the organisation; those in the second category have strong long-term income-generating track records and are valued brands. The third category products will generally carry high hopes for the future – potential replacements for the second category products – while the fourth category contains products either about to fall off the product range, kept on as marginal contributors to overheads, or which are being held awaiting the withdrawal of a weaker competitor from the market.

While it is obviously important for a multi-product company to have a product portfolio when trading in the domestic market, this importance is greatly enhanced in the more complex environment of trans-national trading, with its much larger number of variables. Using appropriate market entry product strategies is the best starting point for ensuring the appropriate spread of risk is obtained.

18. Sales strategies and practices

In this final chapter, we will be looking at the last step in the process of marketing to the public sector and industry in Europe – getting the product sold in the target market. Concentrating on the two aspects of a successful sales strategy, price and quality, we begin by looking at the specific impact the 1992 programme will have on pricing, before moving on to a more general consideration of pricing strategies that are right for your company, and how they inter-act with the market entry strategies investigated in Chapter 15. The chapter then closes by looking at the various ways in which product quality affects the success of export sales, including customer care and after-sales support.

The effect of the 1992 programme on pricing policies

At present, the prices for the same product can vary widely from one EC market to another. For example, prices of pharmaceuticals have a spread across the EC of up to 600 per cent. There are a number of specific results of such wide price variances across a relatively small geographical location, the most major of which are discussed below.

Prices artificially held up

The 1992 programme should in general push prices downwards by opening up public procurement contracts, harmonising technical standards, attracting foreign investment, thus increasing competition, and intensifying competition through market consolidation. The extent of this downward pressure on prices has been estimated by the Commission to be up to 8.3 per cent across all goods and services, although obviously the extent of downward pressures (if any) will vary from industry to industry. A good example of an industry currently under strong pressure by the Commission to lower its prices is the

Airlines

airline passenger business, where a number of pricing cartels have been held as invalid in rulings by the European Court of Justice. It has long been widely believed that the airline carriers have been maintaining prices at an artificially high level.

Cross-border shopping

Price differences from country to country can exist for many reasons, including manufacturer pricing policies (different product positioning from country to country), different profit margins taken by distributors and wholesalers, differing value added tax and excise duty rates, and exchange-rate fluctuations. The cumulative effect of such differences in member states that share a common border has led to a high degree of cross-border shopping. Indeed, such was the loss of trade to business in the Republic of Ireland, where a large degree of cross-border shopping goes on with Northern Ireland (where all four of the above factors are present), that the Irish Government passed what was commonly called the 48-hour rule, whereby cross-border purchases would only be permitted back into the Republic if the purchaser could prove that he or she had been in Northern Ireland for a minimum of 48 hours. Such a rule was intended to eliminate the coach- and car-based shoppers who were migrating north for one day, purchasing large amounts of consumer goods, before returning south again. (The Commission has recently ruled that the 48-hour rule is invalid.)

Ireland

The 1992 programme will increase the ease of cross-border shopping by removing the more time-consuming of customs procedures and banning legislation similar to the 48-hour rule. This, coupled with consolidation through mergers and acquisitions between distributors and wholesalers, and the harmonisation of (or, more strictly, the attempts to approximate) excise duties and VAT will make it much harder for manufacturers to maintain price differentials across national boundaries. Exchange-rate fluctuations (in the absence of European Monetary Union) may be the last cause of price differentials to disappear, leaving only high-price capital goods worth the bother involved in cross-border purchasing.

Parallel importing

The purchase by distributors and wholesalers of lower-priced goods in one country for sale in another has arisen because of similar effects to those detailed for cross-border shopping. The price differences have often been large enough to result in a considerable market in certain goods despite the invalidity in some cases of the manufacturers' warranty. At risk to parallel importing have been computer equipment and software and other goods which have low transportation costs; parallel importing is most common in, but not restricted to, the market for finished products, although there are significant markets for parallel importing of raw materials and sub-component parts.

In one analysis, the existence of parallel importing can be seen as a free market adjusting for the inequalities in prices caused by the artificial factors detailed above. In this analysis, the reasons for having a parallel import market should cease to exist as the four factors are gradually removed by the single market programme. While this may be the case in the long term, in the short term distortions are unlikely to vanish overnight because producers will not immediately remove price variations caused by differing product positioning strategies; because the VAT and excise rates are unlikely to be wholly harmonised; because exchange-rate fluctuations are likely to continue for some time; and because producers will maintain discount policies based on bulk purchasing, which will allow larger distributors to pass these on in the form of lower prices to customers. Also to be considered is the continuation of parallel importing of goods from outside the EC, where differential pricing structures may continue to exist.

Price strategies

This is not an appropriate context in which to undertake a detailed review of the theory and practice of price strategies, and readers wishing to investigate the topic in more detail, or who find some of the terminology or assumptions new, are directed to any of the many excellent text books on the subject. In this section, it is our intention to review pricing strategies which are particularly suited to selling to the public sector and industry, particularly where the seller is selling outside his or her domestic market for the first time. In addition, all three of the pressures detailed in the previous section – the overall downward pressure on prices, the existence of cross-border shopping, and the existence of parallel importing – will have an effect on the pricing policies of producers wishing to sell to the public sector and industry in Europe. Some of these effects are discussed under the appropriate strategies. These are likely to be the pricing practices implemented by companies seeking to trade in other member states in the post-1992 market. They are, therefore, also the pricing policies which you will most commonly meet in your domestic market as competition comes in from other EC countries' manufacturers.

Price cutting

This, expressed crudely, is likely to be the most common product pricing policy induced by the changes brought about by the 1992 programme. Utilised aggressively by companies which wish to develop market share in the EC, and defensively by companies wishing to defend their existing domestic market share, price cutting is likely to begin even before completion of the single market, and before the associated cost reductions are realised. As a result, companies with few reserves, drawn into price cutting by the competitive actions of others, should ensure that economies of scale will eventually materialise, within a manageable time scale. Price cutting is likely to be experienced particularly in industries where the customer base is consolidating into fewer, larger organisations with more purchasing clout, such as the transportation, food and drink industries. The pricing strategies detailed below are specific variations on price cutting which are appropriate to differing market conditions.

Cross-subsidising

It is possible for larger organisations which sell high added-value products and which have a strong competitive position in their domestic market to operate, in effect, their own parallel importing scheme by cross-subsidising prices from one market to another EC market. For such a pricing policy to operate efficiently, the supplier must retain strong controls over costs, particularly those associated with selling into the new market, such as transportation and on-site stockholding costs. This process is one of the factors fuelling the increase in mergers and acquisitions between companies having strong distribution networks, as the merger/acquisition has the important effect of bringing new market delivery costs under internal control.

Margin uplift

The largest volume of cross-border purchasing and parallel importing tends to occur within low-price, low-margin product ranges. Accordingly, companies facing the pressure of an increase in such activities post-1992 should consider lifting the average margins achieved, by the introduction of new products at a higher level in the quality scale, thus diluting the volume of total turnover exposed to either problem. Allied to this strategy is the use of product substitution, whereby the general effect of pushing prices down will not be uniform, and suppliers will consequently need to react to product substitution as purchasers shift from one product to another which has experienced a greater reduction in price. Pharmaceutical suppliers, for example, will find that while prices will generally shift downwards as protective public purchasing practices are reduced, this will not happen uniformly. Prescribers will then move to substitute (where possible) a cheaper product for the more expensive one. If the product is highly branded, with a strong degree of customer loyalty, some resistance to this process can be achieved by introducing a clearly local distinction in the product promotion and packaging, insuring to some extent against both product substitution and parallel importing. Although a consumer product, a good example of this is Coca-Cola, whose strong brand name is accompanied by the use of local language and local distributor promotion. This issue clearly illustrates the interconnectedness of product strategies and pricing strategies.

Penetration pricing

Low introductory pricing is likely to be widely experienced as suppliers bring their products to new EC markets. Some companies may even decide to sell into their new market at a loss to achieve market share early on, particularly where the market is competitive and the product is at the Introductory or Growth stage of its life-cycle (in other words, where long-term profitability is assured if market share can be obtained). This pricing policy was used by Lada to enter the British small car market, advertising at prices below those of local and foreign competitors and quickly establishing a credible market share in its particular part of the market. For penetration pricing to be most effective, a number of factors should be present:

- The product should be easily imitated and strong competition after market entry should be almost certain

- Sales volume should increase dramatically as prices are lowered

- It should be possible to achieve economies of scale when the sales volume increases

- The market for the product should not be fragmented and little or no differentiation or customisation should be necessary

Consequently, market penetration pricing policies are unlikely to be employed by companies with high-margin high-profile products aimed at restricted markets.

Skimming

Moving into a market for the first time often provides an opportunity to charge premium prices – the customer has little alternative choice and is prepared to pay for novelty. Most computer, calculator, photographic and hi-fi products are priced at a level to 'skim the cream off' at the Introductory stage of their product life, with prices tumbling rapidly as 'me-too' products enter the market. This pricing strategy is not available to a supplier entering a market for the first time if that market already has other suppliers of similar product, although product differentiation can help by segmenting the market place. Ray Ban sunglasses are a good example of a product which when introduced to the European market by an American manufacturer was able, by product differentiation, to command a premium price, despite the existence of other sunglasses. The IBM PC similarly was initially priced at almost five times its equivalent selling price today, enabling the manufacturer to recover R&D expenditure at an early stage.

Periodic discounts   A variation on skimming is the use of periodic discounts, where the product is generally sold at a high price, but regular and predictable discounts are available to certain users – for example, the reduction in telephone charges at certain times of day. Again, for the supplier wishing to break into a new market, periodic discounting, perhaps to multinational buyers already taking the product in the suppliers' home market, provides a good method of achieving early credible market share.

Pricing within the sales strategy

All of the pricing strategies detailed above are based on the underlying philosophy of acquiring market share in a new market quickly. They are not maintainable long-term pricing strategies, and it is to be expected that, as the effects of the 1992 programme are worked out and industries complete the re-structuring associated with the changes specific to them, companies will return to the price maintenance strategies more familiar to them in their domestic market – acting broadly as price leaders or price followers. Price leaders will continue to set the pace in the market, not just in price terms, but in continued product innovation and in establishing strong customer loyalties. They will lead from the position of a strong market share, a high level of market intelligence and respect within the industry. Price followers will follow in behind the market leader, seeking to defend a smaller market share, and spending most of their marketing resource, not on trying to attack the market leader, but fending off the pack of smaller competitors below. As the market place settles down post-1992 into these more familiar positions, the emphasis will move from attacking market share to defending the newly acquired market share in the newly entered EC markets. At this point, price becomes one element in the overall sales strategy and the other elements – product quality and sales after-care – come to the fore.

In maintaining newly acquired market share in new EC markets, three factors should be considered in addition to price – the sales vehicle, product quality, and after-sales support and customer care.

The sales vehicle

In Chapter 15, reference was made to the various vehicles which can be considered when entering a new EC market place. To maximise the impact of market entry the choice of sales vehicle must correlate with the company's resources and wider intentions. Companies are not restricted to opening branch or subsidiary offices in the target markets, or to starting greenfield manufacturing operations; some of the other options for sales vehicles are detailed below with comments on their appropriateness to marketing to the public sector and industry in the post-1992 environment.

The home-based sales team

As already stated, this form of selling into Europe from a domestic base, favours large capital goods such as aircraft or steel-rolling equipment, and products for which there is a relatively concentrated and well-known customer base. Services, such as digitised mapping, which are not geographically dependent and which require little customer interface except at the beginning and end of the transaction, are particularly suited to small expert sales teams, domestically based, building strong relationships with European (and indeed world customers). Although companies selling products such as these will have a home-based sales team, there will often be an after-sales support staff locally positioned, and these offices may undertake initial sales activities at a low level – qualifying enquiries and representing the company at second-tier sales activities, such as trade fairs and exhibitions. This system is certainly the simplest of all sales vehicles.

Consortium exporting

Rapidly growing in favour as awareness of the potential of the single market grows is the consortium export system, whereby a number of people from individual companies in the same industry get together to set up a marketing organisation to represent their joint interests. Mostly undertaken by small and medium-sized companies, the export consortium is growing in popularity in the food industry and light engineering, where common distribution chains can be constructed, and where customers can be attracted by a one-stop sales approach. This system is often backed by trade associations and government exporting schemes.

One-stop sales

Agents and representatives

Probably the largest sales system to operate in Europe is the traditional agency activity, where a local agent carries the supplier's product in his portfolio and, depending on the cultural and legal position in a particular member state, may offer the supplier many other services as well, effectively acting as the supplier's eyes and ears on the ground, supplying market intelligence and assisting with any local difficulties which may arise. Obviously the most difficult aspect of agency arrangements is selecting the right person in the first place, and industry recommendation is by far the best method of doing this. British embassies, chambers of commerce and trade fairs can also be very helpful sources of recommendations. Careful consideration should also be given to the coverage given to any one agent; the most common error in this regard is to ask one agent to cover a territory, which, if it was in the supplier's domestic market, might be the domain of two, three or more sales managers. By and large, the agency system will be employed by companies which, for some reason or another (low anticipated sales volume, lack of understanding of the market, inability to incur set-up costs), do not wish to locate in a particular market. It is also, allowing for the fact that agents do not have the supplier's interests exclusively at heart (no matter how hard their protestations to the contrary!) a useful method of testing the water in a particular member state before deciding whether or not to locate there fully.

Distributors and wholesalers

These are an extension of the agency relationship: the distributor actually acquires goods on his own account; wholesalers provide warehousing and distribution services. Distributors are particularly used where a product requires some form of differentiated marketing in the target market, or where the supplier company has not enough resource to market the product adequately in the target market. As the distributor shares in these costs, though often subsidised in various ways by the supplier, such a relationship can be particularly useful at the outset of its market entry, when local input into the product launch and early marketing support is vital. The distributor–supplier is a complex relationship, which can become difficult if and when the distributor becomes substantial in his own right, demanding price reductions from the supplier and perhaps product enhancements. But particularly for high-ticket, mid-volume products, such as chemicals or motor vehicles, the relationship can be ideal.

Manufacture under licence

This, together with franchising, provides a method by which a company can extract return from products and services without being directly involved in their production. Payments are usually in the form of royalties and, while there may be an element of technology transfer between the parties, the original manufacturer usually retains the right to any intellectual property rights involved. This sales system is particularly suited to processes such as patent chemicals production which involve a recipe or process which is 'secret', and the use of materials which are not economically transportable over distance. Additionally, companies may well find that approaches will be made to enter into licensing arrangements with companies from lower-cost countries where there is a strong supply of relatively cheap labour and a developed infrastructure, and which will be offering 'turn-key' manufacturing at a cost lower than that involved in starting a greenfield site.

Product quality

Following a successful market entry, the sales thrust of any company that wishes to maintain market share in its new EC market will emphasise the delivery of quality across the total product (the complete range of benefits the customer perceives to have been gained throughout the buying transaction). This is not the same as saying that every product must be at the top of the quality scale – positioning lower down the quality scale is a valid marketing strategy – but the customers must receive the quality they have paid for, inherent in that product. Take the motor car, for example. There was a time when Jaguar, although producing cars at the top of the quality scale, were not producing quality cars. The Mini, on the other hand, was originally produced as a cheaper motoring alternative, but the quality of the product was excellent. This need to maintain quality across the total product has specific implications in two areas.

The choice of sales vehicle

Safeguards

Going back to the options detailed above, it is important to realise that some sales vehicles (consortium exporting, manufacturing under licence) take control of product quality out of the hands of the ultimate supplier to some degree, and that *all* sales vehicles, except the use of branch offices or subsidiaries, take from you, the supplier, control of some aspect of total product quality. It is vital that any arrangements made to sell into a target market contain strong safeguards regarding not only the product, but the manner in which it is sold. Retailing franchises such as McDonald's and the Body Shop have a lot to teach industry in this regard. In retail franchising, almost every aspect of the total product transaction is reduced to agreed procedures which the franchisee will abrogate at his peril. Not only the manufacture of, say, the hamburger to a standard recipe, but its method of presentation, the state of the premises, even the dialogue used by the sales staff are to some degree pre-arranged and controlled. Arrangements between you and your agent, distributor, manufacturer under licence or joint-venture partner should be equally detailed and strictly policed. Field visits should be made regularly and randomly, product quality audits should be undertaken (by independent third parties if this helps the relationship). Market testing should be undertaken regularly to 'dipstick' the customer perception of how your product is being sold on your behalf. Most importantly, there should be clear instructions as to your rights in the event of any aspect of total product quality being materially lost; there is nothing more frustrating than seeing your product being badly sold, and being unable to affect the situation.

After-sales support and customer care

We began Part III of this book by looking at the market-led company. We then looked at the various steps which should be considered by any organisation seeking to sell its product to the public sector and industry in the single European market post-1992. Any organisation which is truly market led will not view the getting of the sale as the end of the process. Far from it. An organisation imbued with the marketing ethos will take the view that obtaining the sale is the least that can be expected from the application of standard procedures and techniques available to all their competitors. The battle, they will say, begins only now. What differentiates them from other non-market-led competitors is not the obtaining of customers, but how those customers are treated after the sale has been made.

The satisfied customer will return by and large to the organisation which formerly satisfied his needs. Satisfied customers recommend other customers. Satisfied customers even pay their bills. The successful market-led company will, therefore, ensure that it has a customer care, or after-sales support system. Rather like the marketing information system, there is no mystique attached to this process. For a small company, the customer-care system might be a simple card with five or six key questions which is filled out for every major customer transaction, covering such areas as:

- Was the product/service delivered on time?

- Was the product installed properly?

- Did the customer request any modifications and were these implemented acceptably?

- Who was the sales manager on this job?

- When should the customer be contacted regarding spares, servicing or a further sale?

In a larger organisation the after-sales support programme may include telephone calls, personal visits, customer questionnaires, product substitution programmes and promotional activities, all prompted by an extensive customer database. But the underlying ethos is always the same – keep the customer satisfied.

Appendices

Appendix 1: Enforcement – legal cases

As we saw in Chapter 5, the present enforcement mechanisms are not as effective as the Commission would wish. Proposals to make enforcement more effective (both at national and Commission level) are now in a draft directive.

The current directives are effective in member states and in differing degrees the national enforcement mechanisms can be used. The European Court can interpret the directives and set precedents. The European Court also hears cases initiated by the Commission against member states, alleging that the state at central, local or public authority level has infringed the rules.

There were nine cases under instruction by the Commission in 1987. By 1988 this figure had grown to forty-five and is still increasing. The number of specialist staff in the Commission has been increased and monitoring and enforcement are now given greater priority.

The cases following highlight important aspects of public procurement policies.

1. *SA Construction and Enterprises Industrielles and others v. Fonds des Routes and others* (Cases 27, 28, 29/86)

This case was considered after referral from a Belgian court which asked:

1. Whether a contractor's financial and economic standing could be assessed only by the criteria in the Directive.
2. If not, then could a contractor's financial standing be assessed by the value of work being carried out at one time?
3. Does the inclusion of an Italian contractor on a recognised register in his home country mean that he should not be asked to fulfil undertakings (about funds and employment size) to the Belgian authorities?

The Court's answer to the three questions were:

1. No. The Directive refers to other unspecified criteria which may be used.
2. Yes. But if such a measure is to be used, it should be made clear in the tender notice or supporting documents.
3. No. Home registration is not a full answer to the standards for the contract set by the Belgian authority.

This case illustrates the degree of discretion left with the awarding authority, provided the tender notice and supporting documents make the conditions clear, transparent, and without any element of discrimination in favour of home nationals.

2. *Commission v. Italy* (Case 199/85)

The Italian authorities were challenged when, in 1978, the Municipality of Milan awarded a contract to construct a plant to recycle waste without publishing a contract notice in the OJ. During 1980 and 1981 the Commission drew this to the attention of the Italian authorities. In 1983 the Commission commenced the formal procedure and asked for the comments of the Italian authorities.

The Commission thought that the replies were unsatisfactory, sent a 'reasoned opinion' to the Italians in March 1984 and received a reply (which the Commission felt was unsatisfactory). The case was referred to the Court in June 1985. (This slow procedure illustrates the reasons for the emphasis on increased speed placed in the new 1989 Directive.)

The case was defended by the Italians as inadmissible and in any case falling within two exceptions allowed by Article 9 – 'protection of exclusive rights (from) a particular contractor' and 'for reasons of extreme urgency brought about by events unforeseen'.

In the event, the contract never commenced, and the Commission argued that the urgency argument should therefore be dismissed. The Commission also argued that other contractors in the Community could have constructed the type of plant needed.

The Court found in favour of the Commission.

3. *Commission v. Ireland* (Case 45/87)

The Irish authorities were challenged soon after a contract for works on a water supply scheme was advertised. The challenge was to the terms of the contract, which used an Irish standard for asbestos cement pressure pipes. One tender was submitted using Spanish pipes but this was rejected.

In this case, because the Commission was able to act at an early stage, they sought an order that the awarding of the contract should be delayed to allow a hearing. An order was made, but was lifted after the preliminary hearing.

A 'reasoned opinion' was sent to the Irish authorities by the Commission in January 1987. The Irish rejected the Commission's argument, saying that the rejected tender had not shown that the Spanish pipes met the Irish standard.

In an interim decision, the Court refused to order that the award of the contract should be suspended pending a full hearing, arguing:

1. That the need for the new water supply for Dundalk should be the primary consideration
2. That if the Irish authorities had acted illegally the disappointed tenderer had scope for action for damages

In the final judgment delivered in 1988, the Court found that the contract specification did mean that Ireland had failed in its obligations. The Court also pointed out that water supplies are not yet included in the scope of public works directives and that the case rested on Article 30 of the Treaty of Rome, which relates to barriers to trade. The case thus became a test of standards rather than public procurement.

4. *Commission v. Italy* (Case 31/87)

The Commission took the Italian government before the European Court to challenge the contract award by an Italian public authority in La Spezia for a new public incinerator.

The argument of substance was that the Italian authority had not advertised the contract in the OJ. The response by the Italians relied, in part, on 'urgency' and the adverse effect on public health.

The case was registered on 18 July 1988 and the Commission asked that the contract procedures be suspended until the case was heard or, at least, until 15 September 1988 (later extended). The important precedent in this case was that the Court agreed to order the suspension.

On 27 September 1988, the Court accepted the Commission argument that the contract was not greatly influenced by unforeseeable urgency and that it should be advertised.

5. *Beentjes v. The Netherlands* (Case 31/87)

Beentjes is an Italian firm which submitted, in 1987, a tender for a public works contract in The Netherlands. Although they submitted the lowest tender, the contract was awarded to another domestic firm in The Netherlands. The awarding authority argued that Beentjes was rejected because it did not have enough specific experience for the proposed work *and* it did not seem capable of taking on any long-term unemployed people.

The case was referred by The Netherlands court to the European Court for rulings on the points in dispute.

The European Court ruled that the terms of the 1971 Works Directive were applicable to this case, and the Dutch authorities could impose tests of qualifications or experience on contractors provided that they were applied without discrimination. A requirement to recruit a proportion of the labour force from people who were unemployed was also acceptable, again provided that it was applied without discrimination. Such a condition should be advertised with the contract and be capable of being implemented by either a local or external contractor.

The 'non-discriminatory' finding is an important precedent, and the case as a whole clarified how far social issues, such as unemployment, are acceptable in the terms of a contract.

Appendix 2: Viewpoints

Comment from the European Commission: interview with David White, Head of the Public Procurement Policy Unit

David White comments on the scope for potential savings:

> 'Absolutely enormous. We have had some studies done to try and calculate this figure and, I as an economist, have frankly a healthy scepticism of that sort of grand calculation. But if you take the estimates that were done in the context of the "cost of non Europe" and you take the upper range of those estimates it comes out, updated to 1989's value, to a figure of 25,000m ecus per year. That is an absolutely stunning figure. It could be too high or it could be too low; quite frankly if it was half of that, if it was a quarter of that, if it was a tenth of that it would be worth the effort. It would be cheap at half the price.'

He went on to comment on the need for better enforcement procedures:

> 'There are two problems at the moment. One of them is that governments like the idea of opening up, but only if others do it too. I'm not going to give away my market if I think that you are not going to give away yours. So we have got to convince suppliers that not only will we put the measures in place but that they will be seen to be applied. Secondly, there is a credibility problem on the side of a lot of bidders. People do not bid for markets that they are not going to win, or where they don't think they have a chance, and by and large in the public procurement sector bidders do not think it worth their while bidding outside their own country. We have got to change their attitudes to that, and that involves credibility. The only way we can make it credible is by having measures that can be seen to be enforced.'

And finally his reasoning on why this is good news for suppliers.

> 'One word – opportunity. Opportunity to exploit the market. If

you have a good product and a good price and good terms. Not just selling to your established market, but breaking into other markets. We have published in the *Official Journal of the European Communities* something in the order of 25,000 calls for tender last year. That's the present rate and it's going up very fast. Now I'm not suggesting that simply looking at the calls for tender and applying for them, like you might fill in a pools coupon, is the way to get orders, but it gives you a database that you can use to explore where the market is, and to line yourself up to attack opportunities and to try to break into other markets.'

Comment from a government department: interview with David Court, in charge of public sector purchasing policy in Northern Ireland, formerly at the Central Purchasing Unit of the Treasury

'I'm sure that many people are saying, well, we've heard this before, it won't have a really great effect on us. I think there are two important points. The first point is: it's not just about public purchasing – it's about a whole approach to purchasing, getting better value for money. It's very important that a company that sources products to get its own end product, gets that product at the lowest possible price. They will have new opportunities and new sources in Europe for lower cost products and that could have a very marked effect on the final cost price of their product. The second point, which is probably equally important, is that the fact that you do not wish to do very much about exploiting the market does not mean that your competitors won't. What you have to consider is what your competitors are going to do and whether they will be seeking new opportunities. I'm getting approaches all the time from continental firms that are interested in selling, and they are going to try very hard. Selling is a business of exploiting opportunities. You may not be successful in finding new opportunities but you've got to find the level of the competition that will be exploiting your market.

'Waiting and seeing is a very risky strategy. You may well find that you have hot competition on your doorstep that is eating away at your market very rapidly. It is much better to pre-empt that and to find out what the competition is, ensure that the products and the services that you supply are competitive and exploit these opportunities, rather than find out the hard way that some of your staple lines are being eroded very, very rapidly by competition that you cannot stave off. Once competition has established itself it's extremely difficult to push back. It's the initial bridgehead that's important in selling. The first few sales are usually crucial for any product.'

But how does he react to the suggestion that the new systems will add to the costs of purchases because of the extra administration costs?

'There has been a lot of talk about the costs of the system and the bureaucracy. There will be extra costs but they will be marginal. What we are talking about is much larger scale purchasing operations that do it on a professional basis. What we will see is an end of the fragmentation that has typified public purchasing in many areas. There will be larger organisations placing bigger contracts who do exploit the markets and will get these savings. I do believe that savings will be achieved.'

Appendix 3: Model tender notices

Supply contracts

This appendix details the information which must be made available regarding supply contracts.

A. Open procedures

1. Name, address and telephone, telex and facsimile numbers of the contracting authority.

2. (a) Award procedure chosen.
   (b) Form of contract for which offers are invited.

3. (a) Place of delivery.
   (b) Nature and quantity of the goods to be supplied.
   (c) Indication of whether the suppliers can tender for some and/or all of the goods required.
   (d) Derogation from the use of standards in accordance with Article 7.

4. Time limit for delivery, if any.

5. (a) Name and address of the service from which the relevant documents may be requested.
   (b) Final date for making such requests.
   (c) Where applicable, the amount and terms of payment of any sum payable for such documents.
   (d) Address to which they must be sent.
   (e) Language(s) in which they must be drawn up.

6. (a) Final date for receipt of tenders.
   (b) Address to which they must be sent.
   (c) Language(s) in which they must be drawn up.

7. (a) Persons authorised to be present at the opening of the tenders.
   (b) Date, time and place of this opening.

8. Where applicable, any deposits and guarantees required.

9. The main terms concerning financing and payment and/or references to the relevant provisions.

10. Where applicable, the legal form to be taken by the grouping of suppliers winning the contract.

11. The information and formalities necessary for an appraisal of the minimum economic and technical standards required of the supplier.

12. Period during which the tenderer is bound to keep open his tender.

13. Criteria for the award of the contract. Criteria other than that of the lowest price shall be mentioned if they do not appear in the contract documents.

14. Other information.

15. Date of dispatch of the notice.

16. Date of receipt of the notice by the Office for Official Publications of the European Communities.

B. Restricted procedures

1. Name, address and telephone, tele-graphic, telex and facsimile numbers of the awarding authority.

2. (a) Award procedure chosen.
   (b) Where applicable, justification for use of the accelerated procedure.
   (c) Form of contract for which offers are invited.

3. (a) Place of delivery.
   (b) Nature and quantity of goods to be delivered.
   (c) Indication of whether the suppliers can tender for some and/or all the goods required.
   (d) Derogation from the use of standards in accordance with Article 7.

4. Time limit on delivery, if any.

5. Where applicable, the legal form to be assumed by the grouping of suppliers winning the contract.

6. (a) Final date for the receipt of requests to participate.
   (b) Address to which they must be sent.
   (c) Language(s) in which they must be drawn up.

7. Final date for the dispatch of invitations to tender.

8. Information concerning the supplier's own position, and the information and formalities necessary for an appraisal of the minimum economic and technical standards required of him.

9. Criteria for the award of the contract if these are not stated in the invitation to tender.

10. Other information.

11. Date of dispatch of the notice.

12. Date of receipt of the notice by the Office for Official Publications of the European Communities.

C. Negotiated procedures

1. Name, address and telephone, tele-graphic, telex and facsimile numbers of the awarding authority.

2. (a) Award procedure chosen.
   (b) Where applicable, justification for use of the accelerated procedure.
   (c) Where applicable, form of contract for which offers are invited.

3. (a) Place of delivery.
   (b) Nature and quantity of goods to be delivered.
   (c) Indication of whether the suppliers can tender for some and/or all of the goods required.
   (d) Derogation from the use of standards in accordance with Article 7.

4. Time limit on delivery, if any.

5. Where applicable, the legal form to be assumed by a grouping of suppliers winning the contract.

6. (a) Final date for the receipt of requests to participate.
   (b) Address to which they must be sent.
   (c) Language(s) in which they must be drawn up.

7. Information concerning the supplier's own position, and the information and formalities necessary for an appraisal of the minimum economic and technical standards required of him.

8. Where applicable, the names and addresses of suppliers already selected by the awarding authority.

9. Date(s) of previous publications in the *Official Journal of the European Communities*.

10. Other information.

11. Date of dispatch of the notice.

12. Date of receipt of the notice by the Office for Official Publications of the European Communities.

D. Pre-information procedures	
1. Name, address and telephone, telegraphic, telex and facsimile numbers of the awarding authority and of the service from which additional information may be obtained.	procedures of the award of the contract(s) (if known).
	4. Other information.
2. Nature and quantity or value of the products to be supplied.	5. Date of dispatch of the notice.
	6. Date of receipt of the notice by the Office for Official Publications of the European Communities.
3. Estimated date of the commencement of the	

E. Contract awards	
1. Name and address of awarding authority.	7. Nature and quantity of goods supplied, where applicable, by supplier.
2. (a) Award procedure chosen.	
(b) In respect of the contracting authorities listed in Annex II, where appropriate, justification in accordance with Article 6(3) and (4) for the use of such procedures.	8. Price or range of prices.
	9. Other information.
	10. Date of publication of the tender in the *Official Journal of the European Communities.*
3. Date of award of contract.	
4. Criteria for award of contract.	11. Date of dispatch of the notice.
5. Number of offers received.	12. Date of receipt of the notice by the Office for Official Publications of the European Communities.
6. Names(s) and address(es) of supplier(s).	

Works contracts

This appendix details the information which must be made available regarding works contracts.

A. Prior information	
1. The name, address, telegraphic address, telephone, telex and facsimile numbers of the contracting authority.	3. (a) Estimated date for initiating the award procedures in respect of the contract or contracts.
2. (a) The site.	(b) If known, estimated date for the start of the work.
(b) Nature and extent of the services to be provided and, where relevant, the main characteristics of any lots by reference to the work.	(c) If known, estimated time-table for completion of the work.
(c) If available, an estimate of the cost range of the proposed services.	4. If known, terms of financing of the work and of price revision and/or references to the provisions in which these are contained.

5. Other information.

6. Date of dispatch of the notice.

7. Date of receipt of the notice by the Office for Official Publications of the European Communities.

B. Open procedures

1. Name, address, telephone number, telegraphic address, telex and facsimile numbers of the contracting authority.

2. (a) Award procedure chosen.
   (b) Nature of the contract for which tenders are being requested.

3. (a) The site.
   (b) The nature and extent of the services to be provided and general nature of the work.
   (c) If the work or the contract is subdivided into several lots, the size of the different lots and the possibility of tendering for one, for several or for all of the lots.
   (d) Information concerning the purpose of the work or the contract where the latter also involves the drawing up of projects.

4. Any time limit for completion.

5. (a) Name and address of the service from which the contract documents and additional documents may be requested.
   (b) Where applicable, the amount and terms of payment of the sum to be paid to obtain such documents.

6. (a) The final date for receipt of tenders.
   (b) The address to which they must be sent.
   (c) The language or languages in which they must be drawn up.

7. (a) Where applicable, the persons authorised to be present at the opening of tenders.
   (b) The date, hour and place of such opening.

8. Any deposit and guarantees required.

9. Main terms concerning financing and payment and/or references to the provisions in which these are contained.

10. Where applicable, the legal form to be taken by the grouping of contractors to whom the contract is awarded.

11. Minimum economic and technical standards required of the contractor to whom the contract is awarded.

12. Period during which the tenderer is bound to keep open his tender.

13. The criteria for the award of the contract. Criteria other than that of the lowest price shall be mentioned where they do not appear in the contract documents.

14. Where applicable, prohibition on variants.

15. Other information.

16. Date of publication of the prior information notice in the OJ or reference to its non-publication.

17. Date of dispatch of the notice.

18. Date of receipt of the notice by the Office for Official Publications of the European Communities.

C. Restricted procedures

1. The name, address, telephone number, telex and facsimile numbers of the contracting authority.

2. (a) The award procedure chosen.

   (b) Where applicable, justification for the use of the accelerated procedure.
   (c) Nature of the contract for which tenders are being requested.

3. (a) The site.
    (b) The nature and extent of the services to be provided and general nature of the work.
    (c) If the work or the contract is subdivided into several lots, the size of the different lots and the possibility of tendering for one, for several or for all of the lots.
    (d) Information concerning the purpose of the work or the contract where the latter also involves the drawing up of projects.

4. Any time limit for completion.

5. Where applicable, the legal form to be taken by the grouping of contractors to whom the contract is awarded.

6. (a) The final date for receipt of requests to participate.
    (b) The address to which they must be sent.
    (c) The language or languages in which they must be drawn up.

7. The final date for dispatch of invitations to tender.

8. Any deposit and guarantees required.

9. Main terms concerning financing and payment and/or the provisions in which these are contained.

10. Information concerning the contractor's personal position and minimum economic and technical standards required of the contractor to whom the contract is awarded.

11. The criteria for the award of the contract where they are not mentioned in the invitation to tender.

12. Where applicable, prohibition on variants.

13. Other information.

14. Date of publication of the prior information notice in OJ or reference to its non-publication.

15. Date of dispatch of the notice.

16. Date of receipt of the notice by the Office for Official Publications of the European Communities.

D. Negotiated procedures

1. The name, address, telegraphic address, telephone, telex and facsimile numbers of the contracting authority.

2. (a) The award procedure chosen.
    (b) Where applicable, justification for the use of the accelerated procedure.
    (c) Nature of the contract for which tenders are being requested.

3. (a) The site.
    (b) The nature and extent of the services to be provided and general nature of the work.
    (c) If the work or the contract is subdivided into several lots, the size of the different lots and the possibility of tendering for one, for several or for all of the lots.

    (d) Information concerning the purpose of the work or the contract where the latter also involves the drawing up of projects.

4. Any time limit.

5. Where applicable, the legal form to be taken by the grouping of contractors to whom the contract is awarded.

6. (a) Final date for receipt of tenders.
    (b) The address to which they must be sent.
    (c) The language or languages in which they must be drawn up.

7. Any deposit and guarantees required.

8. Main terms concerning financing and payment and/or the provisions in which these are contained.

9. Information concerning the contractor's personal position and information and formalities necessary in order to evaluate the minimum economic and technical standards required of the contractor to whom the contract is awarded.

10. Where applicable, prohibition on variants.

11. Where applicable, the names and addresses of suppliers already selected by the awarding authority.

12. Where applicable, date(s) of previous publications in the Official Journal of the European Communities.

13. Other information.

14. Date of publication of the prior information notice in the OJ.

15. Date of dispatch of the notice.

16. Date of receipt of the notice by the Office for Official Publications of the European Communities.

E. Contract awards

1. Name and address of awarding authority.

2. Award procedure chosen.

3. Date of award of contract.

4. Criteria for award of contract.

5. Number of offers received.

6. Name and address of successful contractor(s).

7. Nature and extent of the services provided, general characteristics of the finished structure.

8. (a) Price or range of prices (minimum/maximum) paid.
   (b) The value and the share of the contract likely to be sub-contracted to third parties.

9. Other information.

10. Date of publication of the tender notice in the Official Journal of the European Communities.

11. Date of dispatch of the notice.

12. Date of receipt of the notice by the Office for Official Publications of the European Communities.

Appendix 4: New approach directives – Toy safety: A case study

At the time of writing three directives have been agreed under the 'new approach' to the harmonisation of standards and regulations: simple pressure vessels, construction products, and toy safety. To illustrate the process of making, agreeing and implementing standards, and the business implications arising from this, we will examine the Toy Safety Directive in some detail. We have chosen this example because it raises the necessary issues and does so in a way that is not overly industry specific.

Toys should be safe. That is the fundamental criterion of allowing any product to circulate in the Community but it is of obvious importance in this case. But how safe? Is it possible to draw up a standard (or series of standards) that could cover the range of toys already available, make provision for the introduction of future toys (which are yet to be imagined), and get agreement throughout the EC?

In the 1970s three attempts were made and each failed. In each case it was impossible to approach unanimity on a detailed proposal as required by Article 100 of the Treaty of Rome.

Following the adoption of the resolution of the 'new approach' in 1985, however, negotiations were re-opened on the new basis. The result has been the adoption within two years of a directive covering most of the toy safety area. It has arisen from the agreement to qualified majority voting.

The Directive fell into three parts, each part was voted through on a majority basis, and the pattern of voting changed between member states at each part. A 'new approach' directive can, thus, make agreement possible where previously all attempts had been unsuccessful.

- Transitional arrangements: until a standard is available essential requirements must be satisfied by conforming to a certified model, as above.

- Free circulation: member states are to ensure products conform with the essential requirements and not to impede those that do. Toys bearing the CE mark are to be presumed to conform.

- Safeguard procedure: Member states are required to remove unsafe products. They must inform the Commission which will investigate. Removal that is unjustified in the eyes of the Commission will give grounds for legal action by the manufacturer against that member state.

    Member states are also asked to check samples and report every three years to the EC.

- Standards: The existing British Standard is replaced with the wording of the European standard. In this case the European standard EN 71 (88) parts 1 to 3 was identically transcribed into a new BS 5665 parts 1 to 3, with effect from the first of January 1990.

The Toy Safety Directive illustrates the components common to all 'new approach' Directives. These are:

- Formal title: Council Directive of 3 May 1988 on the approximation of the laws of the Member States concerning the safety of toys. [Directive 88/378/EEC]

- Entry into force: 1 January 1990. (The implementing provisions adopted and published by 30 June 1989.)

- Scope: toys, defined as products or materials designed or clearly intended for use in play by children of less than 14 years of age – with exceptions (adult toys, toys requiring supervision or special circumstances).

- Essential safety requirements: the user of toys and third parties must be protected against health hazards and risk of physical injury when toys are used as intended or in a foreseeable way, bearing in mind the normal behaviour of children. The particular risks covered are physical and mechanical properties, flammability, chemical properties (including toxicity), electrical properties, hygiene, and radioactivity. The degree of risk is to be commensurate with the user or supervisor. Toys for the under-threes to pay particular attention to labels, packaging and instructions to draw attention to risks and advise on their minimisation, and other specific requirements for certain classes of toys.

- Methods of satisfying the essential requirements: a manufacturer has two choices – either to manufacture in accordance with specified standards, or to conform to a model that has been certified as meeting the essential requirements of the Directive. This latter procedure is known as an EC-type examination and will be carried out by a body approved by the DTI in the UK and its counterparts elsewhere in the rest of the EC. A manufacturer can choose any approved body anywhere in the EC. These standards remain voluntary after the introduction of the Directive.

- Attestation: Toys manufactured in line with the above are to be marked with the EC mark, before being placed on the market, whether for sale or free distribution. The toy must also show the name (trade name or mark and address of the manufacturer), and authorised representative in the Community or importer. A dossier of information must also be kept available for inspection.

- Implementation: The Directive is to be implemented in the UK by regulations made under the Consumer Protection Act 1987 and the European Communities Act of 1972. The Toys (Safety) Regulations of 1974 will then be revoked.

- Responsibility for enforcement will be with the trading standards departments of local authorities in Britain, district councils in Northern Ireland, and responsibility for the national legislation will remain with the DTI, as at present.

That then is the Directive, as it has been formally adopted.

What will happen next? There will be additional parts of the EN (the European Standard) and in turn the British standard to cover chemical toys, such as chemistry sets, and other areas, such as solvents and plastics.

Toy manufacturers may also, depending on their product line, have to conform with other directives. For example, mains voltage toys have to conform with the Low Voltage 1973 Directive. Others will follow: one is expected on 'dangerous imitations' so that toy food is not too realistic, and so on.

To get rid of stock produced before 1 January 1990, the DTI will permit the sale of such stock (without CE marking) to continue until 1 February 1991. This provision for an extra Christmas and January sale follows strong lobbying from the toy industry.

Finally, there will be a general review of progress and problems in 1993 and the process of legislation may start again at that time.

The key points to note are these:

- Be aware of what's happening – it could be your industry next.

- Make sure you know about all the directives that may affect you (would all toy manufacturers recognise the significance of a directive entitled 'dangerous imitations'?).

- Identify now your testing and certification requirements – there will be (industry specific) queues as each directive is adopted.

- Check your information records are up to scratch.

- Take part in standards making – load the dice in your favour.

- Lobby the DTI – they will listen to a reasoned argument.

- Keep your eye on the market.

- Be prepared to fight.

Appendix 5: PowerGen: A case study

PowerGen will, after flotation, be one of the largest privately owned electricity generating companies in the world. The following case study provides a brief overview of one large organisation's approach to the procurement issue. PowerGen illustrates how the procurement issue can and must be integrated into wider management strategy in order to allow it to play an enabling, and not a disabling, role in business strategy. The keys to the PowerGen approach have been information and preparation and, to this extent, they typify a 'market-led' organisation.

Procurement in PowerGen is carried out at corporate level by the procurement department and at local level by administrative officers or other nominees at the appropriate power station site. The scope of procurement includes placing orders and contracts for R&D, consultancy and services; materials and equipment; repairs and maintenance; and new generating plants and projects. Fuel purchase and fuel transport is carried out by specialist staff in the commercial department.

The projected annual spend on procurement of goods and services is expected to be approximately £300 million. This figure does not include any major expenditure which would be occasioned by construction projects such as CCGT stations and the installation of FGD at major coal-fired stations. Procurement is one of PowerGen's best tools in the fight to produce low cost electricity both from an external point of view (the value for money and quality criteria demanded of suppliers) and from an internal point of view (the increase in internal procurement efficiency, such as the use of computerised information and ordering systems, and of Electronic Data Interchange to reap full benefit from paperless trading, geared to the optimum exploitation of resources).

PowerGen has moved towards the devolvement of procurement activity through the periodic review of local procurement limits, but only to the extent that this is cost effective and does not result in missed opportunities. Over 90 per cent of purchase orders are placed by location against call-off contracts established by the corporate procurement department or with local or other suppliers. Since the goods and services that are to be bought direct by power stations and by PowerGen vary widely, and a greater responsibility to place orders and contracts is being given to local locations, PowerGen is encouraging approaches from local contractors and suppliers.

High value or specialist orders will continue to be placed by the corporate procurement department. The main functions of the corporate procurement department are to provide power stations and the corporate divisions with:

- A procurement service for high value or specialist goods or services

- Corporate procurement contracts against which local call orders can be placed

- Specialist procurement support services for corporate and local procurement activity.

Corporate procurement falls into two groups. Supply-only contracts are dealt with by the general purchasing branch and can cover proprietary spares manufactured by the original equipment manufacturer, aggregated programme repairs for repair and maintenance work, general stores items where the aggregated demand brings price discounts and administrative savings. Service contracts are dealt with by the engineering and service contracts branch, covering the repair and maintenance of plant and equipment with associated spares where such an approach results in cost and time savings.

The three key goals for the PowerGen supplier are competitive prices, reliability and high quality. The challenge for any company of PowerGen's size is in maintaining this 'total' approach to procurement given the complex logistics involved. So many individuals are involved in the range of procurement activities, and the activities are themselves scattered across such a wide range of locations, that PowerGen have set up an infrastructure to act as a resource for the procurement function – a division known as management procurement systems and services. For PowerGen, computer systems and procurement procedure guidelines are the leading edge of their support structure, but a long-term, strategic view is also taken, with policy formulation and legislative expertise brought into play. The development of personnel language training and management development are important aspects of their strategy.

The question of procurement and its implications for the cost-effective production of electricity has occupied PowerGen for some time. PowerGen see their responsibility as the identification and exploitation of the best commercial opportunities in order to provide the best service at the best price. The variety of operations (major construction, specialised engineering commission, repetitive purchases of non-specialist equipment) plus the variety of supplier relationships (contractors and sub-contractors) not only make the support services essential but also dictate a variety of solutions. PowerGen are aware of the differing impact of these various factors upon suppliers of different sizes and are actively encouraging smaller suppliers to seek business with PowerGen. However, suppliers need to be aware of all the technical, legal and administrative issues that may affect their work. Local companies, or local distributors of larger companies, may have a leading edge where the logistics of the supply chain dictate. PowerGen is seeking the correct commercial answers, however, and the internationalisation of industry both through joint ventures and mergers and through the complexity of certain manufacturing processes will increasingly dictate international solutions.

PowerGen has identified two main challenges in this area. First is the need to identify the right supplier for a given operation. This process must be confronted by all entities hoping to establish costeffective, quality solutions. Repetitive work and specialist work have very different demands, but the base-line is effective and accurate communication skills with the market place, in this instance, the market place of suppliers. For PowerGen there is a restricted number of possible suppliers of the high level of technological expertise necessary for specialist work. These suppliers are themselves international and very aware of market demands. Some companies may need to examine their communications policies to reinforce their credibility in the procurement market place. Secondly, suppliers must be brought to know the parameters that they must attain to be successful in the scramble for procurement. PowerGen is actively developing systems which comply with EC legislation to ensure that they are advertising their procurement activity early enough and widely enough. The open nature of the procurement market thus established should be a spur to suppliers to identify opportunities more aggressively.

The key to this is the correct identification of business opportunities at an early date by the supplier and the attainment of the necessary high standards in their fulfilment. This is a challenge to the strategic marketing function, bringing buyers and sellers of goods and services together in an appropriate manner. An interesting management development has been to set up one central interface between PowerGen and its suppliers. This investigative procedure identifies opportunities in areas of activity where contracts can be set up allowing PowerGen to call off items and/or services required on a repetitive basis. Such contracts would be 'permissive', allowing locations to choose whether or not to purchase against the contract or use another source, or 'mandatory', where the exclusive use would bring significant benefits to PowerGen.

PowerGen monitor supplier quality for contract compliance and product conformity through their supplier quality branch. A system of in-works inspection and supplier technical assessment is also used. Assessment of potential suppliers varies according to the value and nature of the potential business. For small firms wishing to supply goods and services to local stations, competitive pricing and prompt delivery are priority factors; for larger and more complex requirements a commercial, technical and quality assessment may be required involving an in-depth investigation of suppliers' works and management.

The nature of this assessment means that there will be winners and losers. Even those who do succeed will not be guaranteed a place on the tender lists for any particular project. PowerGen is seeking to maintain a balance between a widening supplier list and a reduction in the administrative problems associated with the placing of orders and contracts.

Appendix 6: Kilco Chemicals: A case study

Kilco Chemicals, a company specialising in the manufacture of high quality hygiene products for the agriculture, dairy, food and brewing industries, employs sixteen people in a plant outside Belfast. Kilco now has a range extending to some 120 products, most of which are tailored to specific client needs and which thus offer a complete protective hygiene system to industry. Kilco also researches, develops and produces own brand products by request from other companies. Their annual turn-over is in the region of £1.5 million and their main markets have traditionally been Northern Ireland, the UK and the Republic of Ireland.

In 1967 Kilco developed a product, Lanodip, a teat dip designed to help control the spread of mastitis in the dairy cow herd. They were successful in patenting this in twenty-two countries.

In common with many small companies which are not hugely resourced, Kilco concentrated on their traditional markets and built their export profile slowly. They thus demonstrated a healthy suspicion of export potential and an understanding of the need to establish a planned growth profile. They began to sell to The Netherlands in a small way in 1976. Kilco had a number of contacts there and used their local networking capacity to achieve a good sales profile. This was due not only to the excellence of Lanodip but also to the accessible nature of the Dutch market, which has similar formalities to those in the UK.

Kilco were already selling in The Netherlands by the time the Dutch authorities issued a 'licence of right', which acted as a crude form of national standard and satisfied the safety requirements of the Dutch market. This licence was renewed on an annual basis and allowed the minor changes requested by the Dutch authorities to reflect changing health standards. A full licence has now been granted by the Dutch authorities to Kilco covering the manufacture and the sale of the product in The Netherlands. Having established a solid base in the Dutch market, Kilco then turned, when requested, to developing a highly concentrated product for the Swedish market. This, too, was highly successful.

Success in the Dutch and Swedish markets led Kilco to turn their attention to expanding their market profile elsewhere in Europe and they identified France and West Germany, both with a large number of dairy herds, as having the greatest market potential for their product. It is at this point that, in spite of the excellent preparatory work undertaken by Kilco, they came up against some of the more intransigent barriers that can be encountered in cross-border selling. Kilco have approached this with a pragmatic sense of what can be achieved and they stand as an example to other companies reaching into new markets where technical regulations play a part.

They established a marketing strategy based around a project team whose job was to explore the German regulations in the field and the optimal way to market Lanodip, using their full knowledge of local particularities. A similar strategy was adopted for France. These teams identified that the immediate goal should be to acquire from the German Health Authority, the BGA, and the French equivalent, the appropriate consents for the manufacturing and sale of the Lanodip formulation. The team comprised a German government vet, a professor of milk hygiene with Munich University, and a representative of the British Consulate in Munich assisted by the Industrial Development Board. The team illustrates the use of local expertise where possible. Kilco had also successfully approached (LEDU) for financial assistance to commence the approval procedure.

The approach in France was similar. The German team decided after the necessary research that a product similar to Lanodip but adjusted to take account of lower iodine levels and different biodegradability levels in West Germany should be submitted for approval.

A two-stage procedure exists in the UK to gain such approval. The DHSS provides the manufacturing licence which testifies to the suitability of the premises and the manufacturing processes. The cleanliness, the quality control and equipment are closely examined and if they reach the required standard the go ahead for production is given. The product then requires a veterinary product licence, issued by the Ministry of Agriculture, which is based upon the submission of the results of rigorous tests and ensures that the product does its job and has no side-effects. The manufacturing licence is widely accepted in Europe but approval for the production of individual product formulations has proved to be difficult in countries other than The Netherlands. This was particularly so in the case of West Germany. (Kilco have been successful in gaining the necessary approvals for the French market.)

Several strongly held national perceptions in West Germany were going to affect the procedure, mainly the environmental bias to legislation. These are perfect examples of natural barriers to market entry. After identifying the strength of the green lobby in Germany Kilco worked hard to produce a formulation that met the companies' needs and proved the product to be biodegradable and environmentally friendly. This required a great deal of toxicological information on the detergent used in the product, most of which had to be sourced in the USA. Technical requirements obviously played a role here, as they did in other areas such as cow fertility.

Nine separate submissions had to be made to the appropriate authorities. The cost to the company of these submissions (including fees to the USA research establishment, consultancy and travelling fees) to certify as safe a product that they had been successfully marketing for sixteen years was over £15,000. The final product differs from the original formulation but not in major respects.

Administrative and organisational problems have dogged the application. There have been significant delays in agreeing the formulation even after the above steps had been taken, as a result of a 'backlog' of work slowing up the processing. Through the IDB, the British ambassador in Bonn and the Ministry of Agriculture, it was finally established that if economic dependence upon the product could be proved, the application would be considerably speeded up. The necessary agreements have not yet been acquired and no date for the marketing of Lanodip can be set as yet. Kilco have been assiduous in complying with both the technical and administrative requirements and still find themselves with no market outlet under their own name in West Germany.

The interesting point from a marketing point of view is that the ultimate delay depended on factors other than the technical formulation of the product. This has the effect of altering the company's perception of the trading conditions in Germany. In their own words, 'Before we started this we thought the German businessman was a slick individual. Now our feelings are very different.' There is, thus, both a practical side to the problem and a psychological side. The difficulties of exporting are compounded by the expectations that these kinds of delay engender. The delays are not always based on reasonable demands but often on bureaucratic formalities and organisational structures that were not designed to facilitate cross-border trading.

An interesting footnote to this case reinforces the above statements. It came to light that Kilco have in the past and still receive royalties from West Germany for the original Lanodip formulation from Beecham, which markets the product in Germany under their own label.

The problems encountered, or similar ones, could have occurred in attempting market entry to any European or world market. This case study is not intended to pick out West Germany as a special culprit. The point must be understood that, even with careful preparation, Kilco came up against barriers of a regulatory, social and administrative nature. They have not yet, as far as the German market is concerned, been 100 per cent successful, but they would have fallen at the first hurdle without this preparation.

Appendix 7: BSI standards policy committee groups

Council for Building and Civil Engineering
Construction department: R. Harrison, Group Manager

BDB/-	Basic Data and Performance Criteria for Civil Engineering and Building Structures	ECB/-	Elements and Components (of diverse materials) for Buildings
CAB/-	Cement, Gypsum, Aggregates and Quarry Products	FHB/-	Farm and Horticultural Buildings
		FRB/-	Fibre Reinforced Cement Products
CLB/-	Clay and Calcium Silicate Products	RDB/-	Road Engineering
CSB/-	Civil Engineering and Building Structures	SEB/-	Building Services
		TIB/-	Timber

Chemical and Health Council
Chemical department: M. J. Pater, Group Manager

ACD/-	Adhesives	LBC/-	Laboratory Apparatus
CIC/-	Chemicals	PTC/-	Petroleum
DAC/-	Dairying	PVC/-	Pigments, Paints and Varnishes
EPC/-	Environment and Pollution	SFC/-	Solid Mineral Fuels
FAC/-	Food and Agriculture	SRC/-	Surface Coatings (other than paints)
HCC/-	Health Care Standards Policy	WPC/-	Wood Preservation

Engineering Council
Mechanical department: A. K. Tidmarsh, Group Manager

ACE/-	Aerospace	MQE/-	Mining and Quarrying Requisites
AGE/-	Agricultural Machinery and Implements	MTE/-	Machine Engineering and Hand Tools
AUE/-	Automobile	NCE/-	Nuclear Engineering
GME/-	General Mechanical Engineering	PSE/-	Piping Systems Components
GSE/-	Gas	PVE/-	Pressure
MCE/-	Machinery and Components	RHE/-	Refrigeration, Heating and Air Conditioning
MHE/-	Mechanical Handling	WEE/-	Welding

British Electrotechnical Committee and Electrotechnical Council

Electrical department: L. G. Roth, Group Manager

CIL/-	Cables and Insulation	LEL/-	Light Electrical Engineering
ECL/-	Electronic Components	LGL/-	Electrical Illumination
EEL/-	Electronic Equipment	PCL/-	Industrial Process Measurement and Control
GEL/-	General Electrotechnical Engineering	PEL/-	Power Electrical Engineering

Council for Multitechnics

Multitechnics department: M. S. T. Langton, Assistant Director (BSI Manchester)

CPM/-	Cinematography and Photography	PLM/-	Plastics
FHM/-	Furniture and Household Equipment	PSM/-	Personal Safety Equipment
FSM/-	Fire Standards Policy	RPM/-	Refractory Products
ISM/-	Iron and Steel	RUM/-	Rubber
NFM/-	Non Ferrous Metals	TCM/-	Textiles and Clothing
PAM/-	Packaging and Freight Containers		

Council for Automation and Information Technologies (T/-)
Restructuring of Information Systems Council (S/-)

Information systems department: P. S. Wells, Group Manager

AMT/-	Advanced Manufacturing Technology	TCT/-	Telecommunications
DOT/-	Information and Documentation	QMS/-	Quality, Management and Statistics
IST/-	Information Systems Technology		

Appendix 8: Bibliography

General references

European File, 'Opening up public procurement in the European Community', January 1989

European Documentation, 'Public procurement and construction: towards an integrated market', 2nd edition, July 1988

Cecchini, P., *The European Challenge: 1992 – The Benefits of a Single Market*, Wildwood House, 1988

Specialised references

Atkins, W. S., *et al.*, *The Cost of Non-Europe in Public Sector Procurement* (2 vols), 1988 (Volume 5 in the Commission sponsored research series)

COM(89)141. Proposal for a Council Directive amending Directive 71/305/EEC concerning the co-ordination of procedures for the award of public works contracts, 4 April 1989

COM(88)376. Communication from the Commission on a Community regime for procurement in the excluded sectors: Water, energy, transport and telecommunications, 11 October 1988

COM(88)377. Proposal for a Council Directive on the procurement procedures of entities providing water, energy and transport services, 11 October 1988

COM(88)378. Proposal for a Council Directive on the procurement procedures of entities operating in the telecommunications sector, 11 October 1988

Advisory committee for public procurement. Amended proposal for a Directive on the coordination of the laws, regulations and administrative provisions relating to the application of Community rules on procedures for the award of public supply and public works contracts (CC/89/02), 2 January 1989

Advisory committee for public procurement. Public procurement in the field of services: field of application of an EC-directive (III/7106/89), 13 January 1989

Advisory committee for public procurement. Consolidation of the supplies Directives (CC/88/31), 15 November 1988
British Gas, Position paper and critique of proposed Directive on procurement procedures (as published in COM(88)379), October 1988

Cometec-Gaz. Views of Cometec-Gaz on the proposal for a Directive on procurement procedures, 19 May 1989

Confederation of British Industry, 'Liberalising public procurement in the EC; preparing for 1992', Brief No. 7

Confederation of British Industry Parliamentary Brief, 'Procurement in the Excluded Sectors', House of Commons, 16 May 1989 (with supplementary paper on the role of audit in public procurement)

European Commission, 'Working paper on remedies in the field of public procurement in member states of the Community' (DG III/F/7086), 8 December 1988

Foot, A., '1992: Contracting in the European Market, Problems for Buyers', Paper presented at the Institute of Purchasing and Supply Conference, 23 September 1988

General Agreement on Tariffs and Trade, Agreement on Government Procurement (and annexures), 1988

H.M. Treasury, 'Guidance notes on public sector purchasing international obligations', 1988

H.M. Treasury, 'Public purchasing policy: consolidated guidelines', 1988

H.M. Treasury, *Explanatory memoranda*: On proposed enforcement directive (13 October 1987); On proposed amended works directive (25 July 1988); On proposed directive on excluded sectors (18 November 1988); On proposed enforcement directive (13 February 1989); On proposed amended works directive (26 April 1989); On proposed enforcement directive (2 May 1989); On proposed directive on excluded sectors (10 May 1989)

Porter, M.E., *Competitive Strategy*, Macmillan, 1980

Woolcock, S., *Making a reality of the single European market: public procurement*, RIIA, 1989

Appendix 9: Contact points

Contract notices

Details of supplies and works contracts to be let by central, regional and local government will be published in the supplement to the *Official Journal of the European Communities*. This is obtainable on subscription, or individual copies may be obtained from HMSO or their sub-agent at the addresses below:

HMSO Publications Centre   Alan Armstrong (sub-agent)
51 Nine Elms Lane   2 Arkwright Road
London SW8 5DR   Reading RG2 0SQ
(Tel: 071–873 8409)   (Tel: 0734 751769)

The contract notices are also available through TED (Tenders Electronic Daily), a computerised system which may be accessed through a number of host organisations. TED is run by:

Office for Official Publications of the European Communities
Sales Department
L-2985 Luxembourg
(Tel: 010–352 499281; RELEX: 1324 PUBOFLU; Fax: 010–352 490003)

The DTI's Export Intelligence Service (EIS) now includes tender opportunities direct from TED as an element in its own computerised system, designed mainly to give exporters advance warning of any trade opportunities in their markets and products. Any firm which exports UK goods or services can subscribe.

A daily commercial service is also provided by:

European Contract Information
Glasgow University Library
Hillhead Street
Glasgow G12 8QE
(Tel: 041 339 8855, extension 6740/6797)

Centres for European Business Information

The European Commission has established the Euro-Info network in partnership with other organisations which offer support to small businesses. They stock the OJ and are linked to TED.

Birmingham
Chamber of Industry and Commerce
PO Box 360
75 Harborne Road
Birmingham B15 3DH
(Tel: 021 454 6171)

Glasgow
Scottish Development Agency
21 Bothwell Street
Glasgow G2 6NR
(Tel: 041 221 0999)

London
Department of Employment
Small Firms Service
Ebury Bridge House
Ebury Bridge Road
London SW1W 8QD
(Tel: 071–730 8115)

Newcastle
Documentation:
Polytechnic Library
Ellison Place
Newcastle upon Tyne NE1 8ST
(Tel: 091 232 6002)
Administration:
Northern Development Co. Ltd
Bank House
Carliol Square
Newcastle upon Tyne NE1 6XE
(Tel: 091 261 0026)

Firms wishing to be put in touch with their nearest centre should contact the Small Firms Unit (dial freephone 100 and ask for Freephone Enterprise)

Contents and progress of EC legislation

The DTI's Hotline number is 071–200 1992.

The Spearhead database includes texts of adopted directives and is accessible through the Profile Information Service, Telecom Gold, Mercury Link, Electronic Mail Services, IRS Dialtech and One to One. Further details are available from the DTI's 1992 Hotline.

Technical standards

Technical standards are appearing at an increasing rate and are affecting more and more areas of manufacture. There is a Standards Action Plan for Business produced by the DTI which can be contacted through the DTI's 1992 Hotline. It is also accessible via Pergamon Financial Data Services. Details are available from 081–993 7333.

The British Standards Institute can be contacted at:

BSI
Linford Wood
Milton Keynes MK14 6LE
(Tel: 0908 220022)
(For Subscriptions, Library and Technical Help for Exporters, Standards Sales, Tel: 0908 221166)

Otherwise use individual BSI contacts for each product (see Appendix 7).

The International Standards Office can be reached at:

International Standards Office
Rue de Varenne 1
Boîte Postale 56
CH 1211
Geneva
Switzerland

The local DTI office offers advice on the 1992 programme and the effect it will have on industry. The local offices are as follows:

DTI East (Cambridge)
Building A
Westbrook Research Centre
Milton Road
Cambridge CB4 1YG
(Tel: 0223 461 939)

DTI East Midlands
Severns House
20 Middle Pavement
Nottingham NG1 7DW
(Tel: 0602 506181)

DTI North East
Stanegate House
2 Groat Market
Newcastle upon Tyne NE1 1YN
(Tel: 091–235 7270)

DTI North West (Manchester)
Sunley Tower
Piccadilly Plaza
Manchester M1 4BA
(Tel: 061–838 5227)

DTI South East (Reading)
40 Caversham Road
Reading RG1 7EB
(Tel: 0735 395600)

DTI South West
The Pithay
Bristol BS1 2PB
(Tel: 0272 272666)

DTI Yorkshire & Humberside
Priestley House
3–5 Park Row
Leeds LS1 5FL
(Tel: 0532 443171)

DTI North West (Liverpool)
Graeme House
Derby Square
Liverpool L2 7UP
(Tel: 051–227 4111)

DTI South East (London)
Bridge Place
88–9 Eccleston Square
London SW1V 1PT
(Tel: 071–215 0576)

DTI South East (Reigate)
Douglas House
London Road
Reigate RH2 9QP
(Tel: 0737 226900)

DTI West Midlands
Ladywood House
Stephenson Street
Birmingham B2 4DT
(Tel: 021–631 6181)

In Northern Ireland, Scotland and Wales, the contacts are:

Industrial Development Board
IDB House
64 Chichester Street
Belfast BT1 4JX
(Tel: 0232 233233)

Welsh Office
Cathays Park
Cardiff CF1 3NQ
(Tel: 0222 825111)

Scottish Office
Alhambra House
45 Waterloo Street
Glasgow G2 6AT
(Tel: 041–248 2855)

Index

acquisitions, 83, 90–1, 93, 120–1, 125, 130, 135, 150, 152
advertising, 22, 29–31, 44, 46, 109, 128, 153, 164–6
aerospace products, 4, 6, 8, 12, 79, 188
after-sales support, 155, 158–9
agents, 156
agricultural and industrial machinery, 8, 15
Agriculture, Ministry of, 185–6
AIM (Advanced Informatics in Medicine), 147
aircraft equipment, 16, 143–4, 155
Amstrad, 129
ANFOR, 53, 71
Anglepoise, 129
annual reports, 109
Apple Macintosh, 129
architecture, 44
ASEA, 102
awards
    criteria, 26, 34–8, 43, 170–75
    made under international agreement, 23, 30

barriers to trade, 165, 185, 186
    artificial, 77–82, 84–6, 106
    natural, 77–82, 85–6, 91, 105–6, 117, 134, 138, 141, 185
    see also technical barriers to trade
Beentjes, 35, 166
Benetton, 80
BGA, 185
biotechnology, 146
Black and Decker, 129
Body Shop, 158

branch offices, 122–3, 155, 158
BRITE (Basic Research in Industrial Technologies for Europe), 147
British Aerospace, 6
British Airways, 6
British Gas, 6
British Rail, 97
British Shipbuilders, 6
British Standards Institute, 70–71, 110, 193
    British Standards, 51, 53, 177–8
    standard policy committee groups, 187–8
British Telecom, 6
Brown Boveri, 102
building, 8–9, 12, 15, 17, 28, 44, 56, 60, 187
business services, 9, 12, 15
buying requirements, 91–2

CAD/CAM, 147
'cassis de Dijon', 64
CBI, 110
Cecchini Report, 7
CEN, 69–72, 74
CENELEC (Comité Européen de Normalisation Electrotechnique), 62–3, 69–72, 74
Centres for European Business Information, 192
chambers of commerce, 109, 111, 192
civil engineering, 8–9, 12, 15, 17, 28, 44, 187
coal, 4, 8–9, 12, 14–15, 40–41
Coca-Cola, 153
communications, 8, 97
Community law, 36, 60, 69, 93

Community law – continued
    see also legal issues; public procurement; Rome, Treaty of
competition, 3–6, 11–12, 16–17, 40, 42, 84–5, 88–91, 95–6, 106, 109, 112, 117–20, 122–6, 140, 148–53, 155, 159, 168–9, 181
competitive advantage, 127–8, 137–8
    in the company, 128–30
    in industry, 134–7
    in the market place, 133–4
    strategies, 130–2
computers, 12, 44–5, 129, 147, 151, 154
    mainframe, 14–15
consortium exporting, 156, 158
contract authorities, 22, 29, 31, 34, 175
Construction Products Directive, 72
cost leadership, 128–30, 137
Court, David, 168–9
cross-border contracting, 27, 35
cross-border selling, 185
cross-border shopping, 150
cross-functional teams, 100, 112
cross-subsidising, 152
culture, 98–103, 111–12, 156
customer care, 155, 158–9

DEC, 102
declining industries, 4, 134, 136
defence, 4, 23, 30
DELTA (Development of European Learning Through Technological Advancement), 147
DHSS, 185
digitised mapping, 155

DIN, 51, 53
'dipstick', 158
distributors, 156–7, 182
Documentation, 192
domestic, local markets, 3–5,
    28, 79–80, 106, 111,
    120–26, 130, 135, 141–2,
    144–5, 148, 151, 153, 156
see also home-based sales team
DTI, 178–9, 193–4
    BOTIS database, 107
    'Brussels Can You Hear
        Me?', 71
    Export Intelligence Service
        (EIS), 107, 192
    'Guide to European
        Community Research and
        Development Programmes,
        A', 147
    Hotline, 193
    offices, 107
    Spearhead database, 193
    Standard Action Plan for
        Business, 193
Dundalk, 165

Economist, The, 109
Economic and Social
    Committee, 41, 74
electricity, electrical products,
    6, 8–9, 12–16, 41, 56–7, 60,
    79, 146, 188
see also Low Voltage Directive
Electronic Data Interchange,
    180
Electronic Mail Services, 192
emerging industries, 4, 134–5
employers' organisations, 110
Employment, Department of,
    192
EN (European Standards), 177–8
energy, 4, 6, 9, 12, 18, 29, 41
Enterprises Industrielles, 163
ENV (European Pre-standards),
    70
ESPRIT (European Strategic
    Programme for Research
    and Development in
    Information Technology),
    121, 147
estate agencies, 92
EUREKA, 147

Euro-Info Centre, 39, 192
Euromonitor, 109
European Commission, 26, 31,
    36–46, 59–66, 68–9, 71–4,
    108, 114, 140–41, 147,
    149–50, 163–5, 167, 177,
    192
European Communities Act of
    1972, 178
European Communities Host
    Organisation (ECHO), 47,
    115
European Contract Information,
    191
European Court of Justice,
    36–7, 64, 69, 150, 163–6
European Free Trade
    Association (EFTA), 47,
    69–71, 114
European Investment Bank, 48,
    115
European 'magic triangle', 133
European manager, 101–2
European Monetary Union, 150
European multinationals, 102–3,
    119, 136
European Parliament, 38, 41,
    65, 74
European Telecommunications
    Standards Institute (ETSI),
    72
European Working Party on
    Standards (EWPS), 72
'excluded sectors', draft
    Directive, 115
exhibitions, 155

finance-led organisations, 98,
    129
financial services, 92, 134, 193
Financial Times, 109
food and drink industries, 56–8,
    79, 92, 129, 152, 156, 187
Ford, Henry, 98
Ford of Europe, 89
'Fortress Europe', 85, 102, 123,
    136
fragmented industries, 134–5
franchising, 157–8

gas, 6, 8–9, 41, 187

General Agreement on Tariffs
    and Trade (GATT), 19, 21,
    23, 47, 114–15
'global highway', 133
global industries, 134, 136–7
green-field operations, 122–3,
    155, 157
Groupe MAC, 56–7

hairdressing, 78–80, 83
Harrison, R., 187
HD (Harmonisation
    Documents), 70–71
health care and social services,
    44, 187
heavy fabrications, 12, 14
HMSO Publications Centre, 191
home-based sales team, 122,
    130, 155
'honeymoon effect', 95–6, 144
Honeywell, 101
hotel and restaurant services,
    44, 129
human health and safety, 57,
    188
hygiene products, 184–6
    see also Lanodip

IBM PC, 154
Industrial Development Board
    (IDB), 185–6, 194
information, 23–4, 28–9, 31, 44,
    105, 116, 119, 127, 131
    basics, 106
    problem areas, 110–11
    sources, 46–8, 107–10
    statistics, 112–13
    see also marketing information
        systems (MIS); public
        procurement
Institute of Directors, 110
Internal Market and Industrial
    Affairs, 39
International Electrotechnical
    Commission (IEC), 70–71
international markets, 79, 139
International Organisation for
    Standardisation (ISO),
    70–72
IRS Dialtech, 193
IT, 102, 147, 188

Jaguar, 158
Japan, 6, 14, 17, 102, 114, 136–7, 140, 147
JESSI (Joint European Semiconductor Silicon Project), 121, 147
joint ventures, 121–2, 125, 130, 158
Jordans, 109

'key account' concept, 90
Kilco Chemicals Ltd, 138, 184–6

Lada, 153
Langton, M.S.T., 188
languages, 10, 110–11, 114, 153, 170–74
Lanodip, 138, 184–6
lasers, 15
La Spezia, 165
lawyers, 80, 83
LEDU, 185
legal cases, 163–6
legal issues, 27, 35, 156, 182
    see also Community law; European Commission; European Court; Rome, Treaty of
legal services, 44
'licence of right', 184
light engineering, 156
Low Voltage Directive, 60, 62, 178

maintenance and cleaning, 45
management consultancy, 44–5
manufacturing under licence, 100, 130, 141, 157–8, 184–5
margin uplift, 152–3
market entry, 90, 99, 130, 132, 139, 145, 153, 155, 157
    assessing market sectors and sizes, 116–19
    holding on at home, 123–6
    strategies, 119–23, 127, 146–9
market-led organisations, 97–8, 158–9, 180
    organisational culture, 98–103
marketing in Europe
    achieving the benefits, 77–9
    categories, 79–80

marketing in Europe – *continued*
    consolidation, 89–91, 101–2, 120, 146, 149–50, 152
    fragmentation, 77–84, 89, 91–3, 95, 153
    research, 9, 93, 95, 103, 105–6, 109, 118, 144
    simple, 88–9
    strategic, 87–97, 99–103, 106, 116, 127, 140, 182
    see also barriers to trade
marketing information systems (MIS), 103–4, 106–7, 113, 159
Marks & Spencer, 80
Marriott Hotels, 129
mature industries, 134–6
McDonald's, 129, 158
media, the, 109
Mercury Link, 193
mergers, 83, 90–91, 93, 102–3, 120–21, 125, 130, 134, 150, 152
Mini, the, 158
Mintel, 109
mobility of labour, 78
Model Tender Notices, 23, 31, 170–75
motor vehicles, 8, 56, 58–9, 78, 80, 83, 92, 113, 153, 158, 187
    see also transportation
mutual recognition, 62–4, 73–4

NACE code, 114
national markets, 3–5, 28, 36, 79–80, 116, 141
'new approach' directives, 62–7, 176
new product development (NPD), 142, 146–7

Office for Official Publications of the European Communities, 170–75, 191
Official Journal of the European Communities (the OJ), 18, 22–3, 25, 29–31, 33, 36, 43, 46, 108, 114, 164–5, 168, 171–2, 174–5, 191–2
oil, 8, 41–2, 79–80, 83, 187
One to One, 193

pan-European company, 120–21
parallel importing, 150–53
Pater, J., 187
penetration pricing, 153
Pepsi, 110–11
Pergamon Financial Data Services, 193
personal services, 78–9
pharmaceuticals, 12–13, 56, 58, 146, 149, 153
Philips NV, 89
PowerGen, 180–83
prices
    cutting, 152
    effect, 11, 16
    policies, 149–50, 152
    strategies, 149–54
    see also penetration pricing
printing and publication, 9, 12–13, 44
product strategy, 153, 157
    building a product portfolio, 147–8
    definitions, 139–40
    for new markets, 142–7
    see also new product development (NPD); technical standards
production-led companies, 97–8
products
    adaptation, 143–4
    differentiation, 129–30, 137–8, 141–2, 154, 157
    elimination, 144–5
    life-cycle review, 145–6
    line extension, 145
    positioning, 142–3, 151, 157
    quality, 143, 155, 157–9
    rejuvenation, 144–5
    substitution, 152–3
    testing, 94–6
Profile Information Service, 193
public health and safety, 29, 60, 65–6, 165
public procurement
    broadening the scope, 40–45
    enforcing the rules, 36–9
    information, 105, 113–15
    local and national preferment, 3–5, 28, 36
    policy, 17–20, 28, 36, 78, 88, 167–8, 180–83

public procurement – *continued*
  see also European
    Documentation
public sector
  definitions, 5–6
  directive, 46, 114
  enterprises, 7, 21, 28, 40–43
  liberalising, 3–9
  potential, 10–20
  purchasing policy, 168–9
  savings, 11–17
  suppliers, 7–13, 18–21, 26, 33,
    36–7, 43, 112–15, 133, 137,
    152–7, 170–72, 175, 181–3
  trading utilities, 22, 29, 40,
    42–3, 46, 114
  value, 6–7
public supplies
  directives, measures,
    principles, 17–19, 42–7,
    114–15
  procedures, 21–7
public works
  directives, measures,
    principles, 17–19, 29, 42–6,
    114, 165–6
  procedures, 28–35

RACE (Research and
  Development in Advanced
  Communications
  Technology for Europe),
  147
Ray Ban sunglasses, 154
recruitment, 101, 123, 166
research and development
  (R&D), 9, 44, 98, 121, 130,
  135, 146–7, 154, 180
restructuring effects, 12–16,
  89–90, 146, 154
retail sector, 79–80
Rome, Treaty of, 36, 39, 58,
  63–5, 165, 176
Roth, L.G., 188

Sacilor, 136
SA Construction, 163
safety, 62, 66–9
  see also human health and
    safety; public health and
    safety

sales
  strategies and practices,
    149–59
  supply chain, 108
  vehicles, 155–8
sales-led organisations, 98
Scottish Development Agency,
  192
Scottish Office, 194
Sealink, 6
service contracts, 40–45
sewage and refuse disposal, 44,
  164–5
Sherpa military aircraft, 143–4
Short Brothers, 129, 143
single market, 3–6, 11, 62,
  88–90, 92, 97, 100, 119,
  123, 141, 152, 156, 158
  see also marketing in Europe
skimming, 154
small contracts, 22–3, 29–30
Small Firms Unit, 192
special security measures, 23, 30
steel-rolling equipment, 155
stockholding costs, 91–2, 122,
  130, 138
strategic alliances, 89–90,
  121–2, 125, 135
Structural Funds, 48, 115
sub-contracting, 47–8, 115, 175
subsidiary companies, 122–3
supply chains (buyers and
  sellers), 130
  see also sales
SWOT analysis, 131

target markets, 28, 99, 111, 139,
  141–2, 144–5, 149, 155,
  157–8
taxes, 78, 117
  see also VAT
technical barriers to trade, 16,
  78, 81, 105
  differential impact, 55–61
  effect, 51, 53–4
  forms, 51–2
technical standards, 5–6, 16,
  51–4, 78–9, 170–74, 185–6,
  193–4
  common, 25, 34

technical standards – *continued*
  harmonisation, 57–74, 101–2,
    110, 118, 139–41, 146, 165,
    176
  see also ANFOR; British
    Standards Institute; DIN;
    EN; HD; International
    Organisation for
    Standardisation (ISO)
Telecom Gold, 193
telecommunications, 4, 6, 12,
  15, 18–19, 41–4, 56, 60–61,
  72, 78, 80, 83, 134, 188
telephone handsets, 15
tendering, 18, 22, 26, 31–2,
  34–6, 43, 164–6
  procedures, 24–5, 29, 32–3
  see also Model Tender Notices
Tenders Electronic Daily (TED)
  database, 22, 29, 46–8, 108,
  114–15, 191–2
Texas Instruments, 129
textiles and clothing, 79, 188
third country businesses, 102,
  123, 131
Tidmarsh, A.K., 187
toy safety, 66, 176–9
trade associations, fairs,
  publications, 109, 155–6
training, 101–2, 123
transportation, 4, 6, 8–9, 11,
  13–16, 18, 29, 41–2, 44,
  78–9, 81, 91–2, 122,
  129–30, 138, 143–4, 150–52
'turn-key' manufacturing, 157

unemployment, 166
USA, 6, 14, 17, 47, 61, 102,
  114, 136–7, 140, 147, 186
Usinor, 136

VAT, 30, 150–51

water, 6, 9, 18, 29, 40–41,
  164–5
Wells, P.S., 188
Welsh Office, 194
White, David, 167–8
wholesalers, 156–7